The first
Alphabet
of painting

Easily learn to draw with letters and numbers

140 learning designs
Yiannis   Kotzapanagiotis

Dedicated to Alexandra, Sofia, Anastasis and Nikolas

Author Yiannis Kotzapanagiotis

Yiannis Kotzapanagiotis is a graduate of the School of Design and Painting ABC DE PARIS.
 He is a member of the international artistic programe Crea Centers with the art of Stained Glass. He has been professionally engaged in painting, glassmaking - stained glass and hagiography, for the last 25 years in his workshop in Kavala Greece.
He visited Mount Athos many times for the Hagiography.
He imparts his knowledge in Painting, Stained Glass and Hagiography to associations, schools, groups, youth centers etc.
He is the author of books about art but has also illustrated books mainly of environmental interest.

He is also involved in the construction of stage sets for theatrical performances and the creation of animation.
Through the summer exhibitions, many of his works have also traveled to many countries

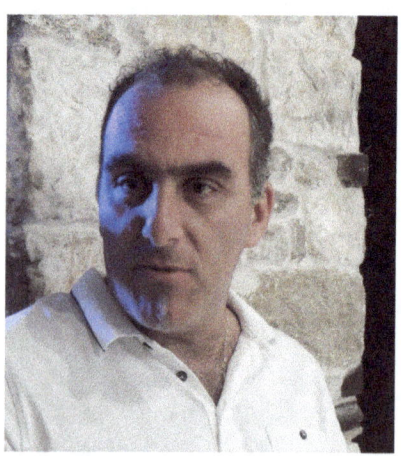

This book is an enriched version of the "First Painting Alphabet" published in Greece by the author himself. The method of drawing step by step from the Greek letters is quite easy for children and beginners. There are also more complex drawing for more advanced artists. In this version there are also colored drawings so that the drawing can be completed slowly with color. All over the world there are very good drawing books by established artists.

This small book is an attempt to give an easy start to anyone who wants to be involved with the visual arts, based on the design of letters and numbers that we all know.

Starting from the design of each letter, everyone can make their own new designs. It's easy!

Now here is the introduction from the original version

A few words instead of an introduction
I have been involved in art since I was a small child and more than 25 years with painting lessons.
I have met remarkable people, who I also learned from them.
I went to other artists, made exhibitions, participated in various actions, created projects, taught art.
The main reason for making this handbook came when I realized
that the fear of drawing was intense among many people.

In the painting lessons I do in collections, schools, groups, etc., I found that while there is a lively interest in visual arts, it is difficult for us to draw, for example, even a small flower. We resort to the solution of photocopying, reduction, enlargement, carbon for very simple things. This whole process is time-consuming and tiring. Also, by simply copying a design, we lose the joy of creating something completely our own.

With a rough assessment of my own, I saw that 80% of people who are involved in art, can comfortably draw, 10% can't at all and 10% are what we call talents. So it's a shame that we can but not have something that will give us the stimulus to start without fear.

So for this reason I made this booklet, so that everyone can draw simple everyday things, animals, plants, people. The step-by-step method is simple and easy to understand. It is based on the letter and number patterns we all know.

So we have a big database ready inside our mind. So by drawing a letter, we can continue it and make a drawing. For examble ,if we need to make a butterfly, we know that we will start by drawing the small Greek letter λ.

If someone (even if they had never drawn before), takes the pencil and continues the design suggested for each letter or number, it is certain that together with the letter the whole design will remain in his mind.

I have worked it on children as well as adults with wonderful results. It is also a starting point for new creations as infinite designs can be made.

Along with the 24 Greek letters there are also the Latin ones that differ, as well as the 10 numbers. Also some color drawings for samples.

Important and without much detail are the references to Shading, Perspective and Color. I think for someone who wants to start with visual arts it is quite an interesting aid. It does not include difficult designs and concepts that would frustrate a beginner. It starts from very easy and goes up to moderately difficult designs. It can also help more experienced artists who struggle at drawing.

Clearly, there are very good art books by excellent artists with a recognized contribution and value to the visual field. It does not replace any other similar book, but it comes to complete a small stone in the search for ways to make the art look simpler and ultimately be embraced by more people.

The "Alphabet of painting" is a book that deserves to be in every home, school, club as a constant source of daily drawings for the child, the parent, the teacher, the artist.

One last thing. Visual arts cultivate kindness in our soul because by creating anything, we feel more useful people. Without patterns and colors our world would be unbearably poor. It is therefore a form of spiritual upliftment for the creator as well.

Have fun

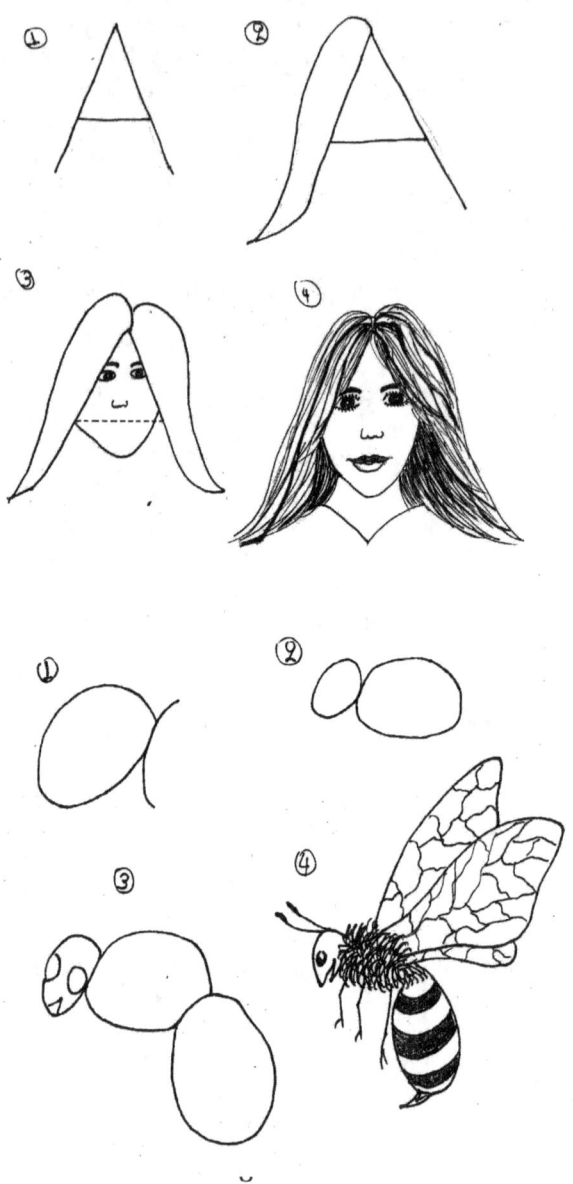

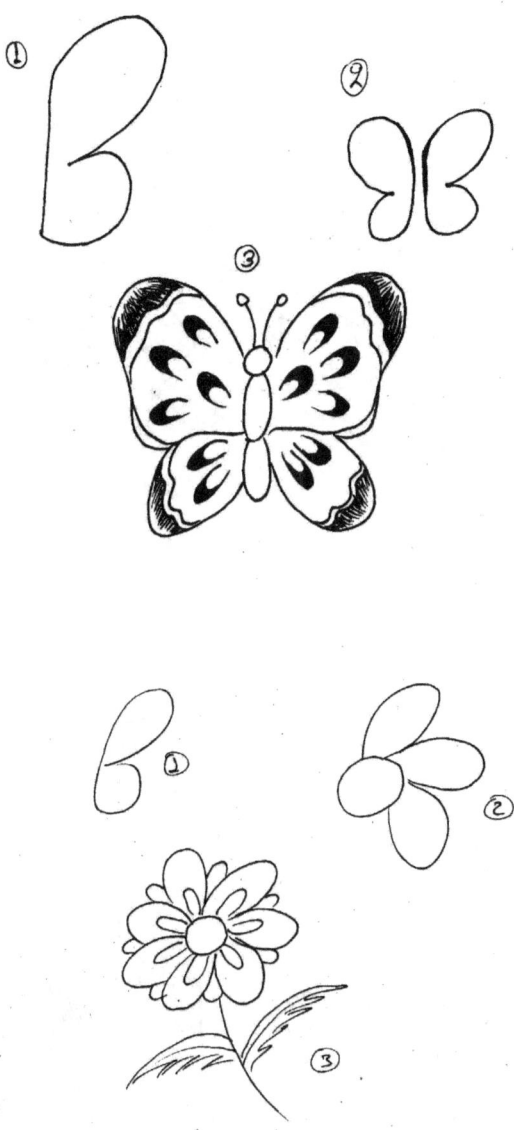

9

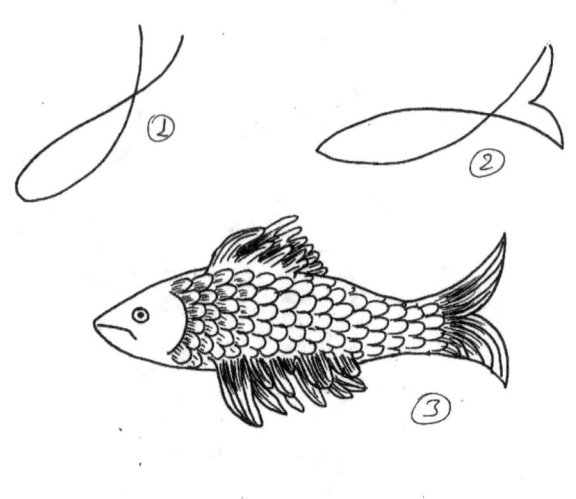

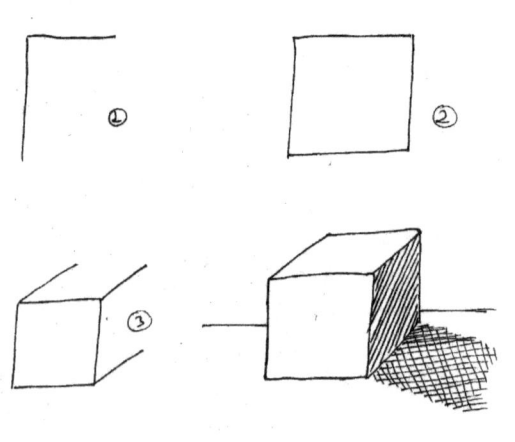

10

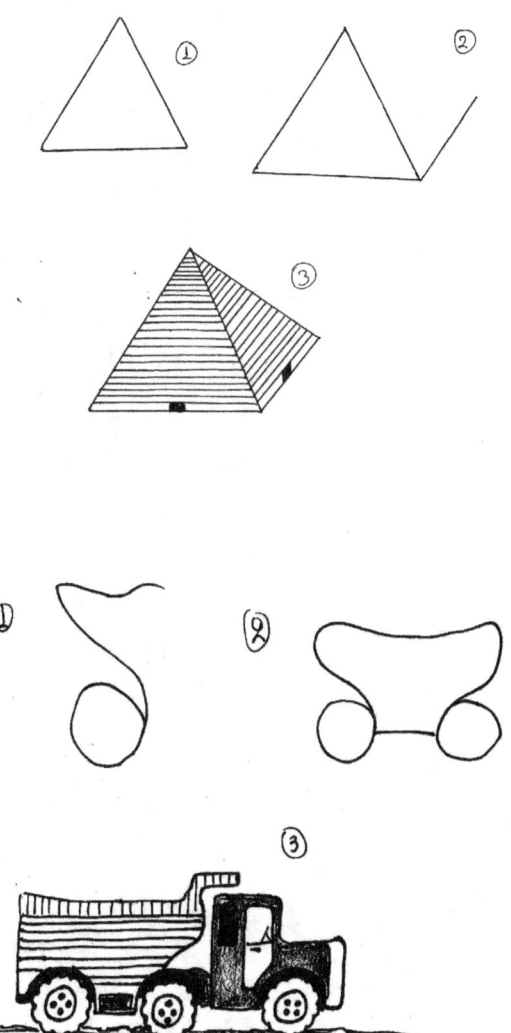

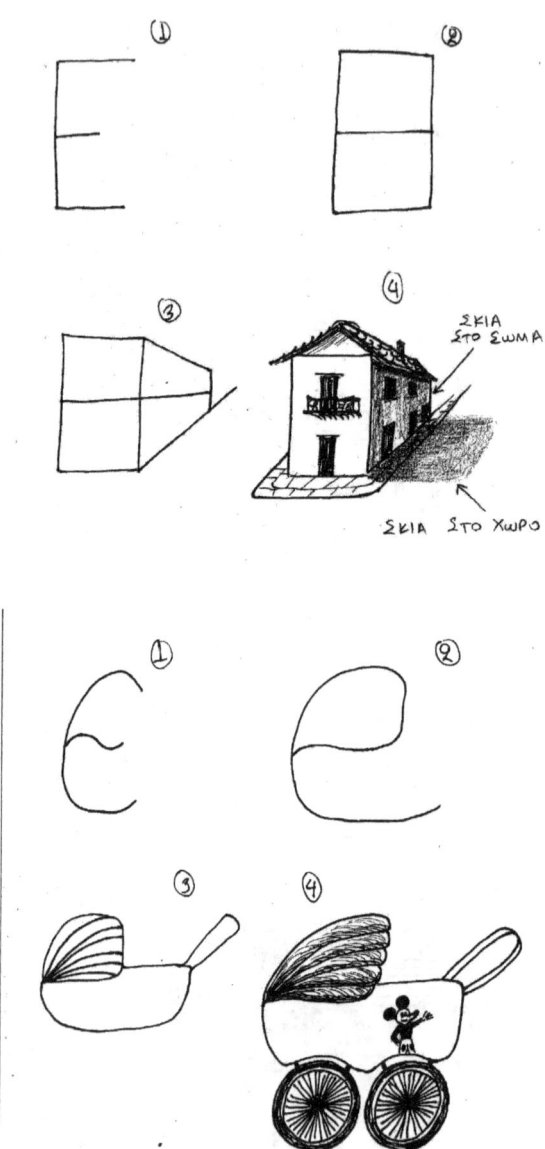

① ②

③ ④ ΣΚΙΑ ΣΤΟ ΣΩΜΑ

ΣΚΙΑ ΣΤΟ ΧΩΡΟ

① ② ③ ④

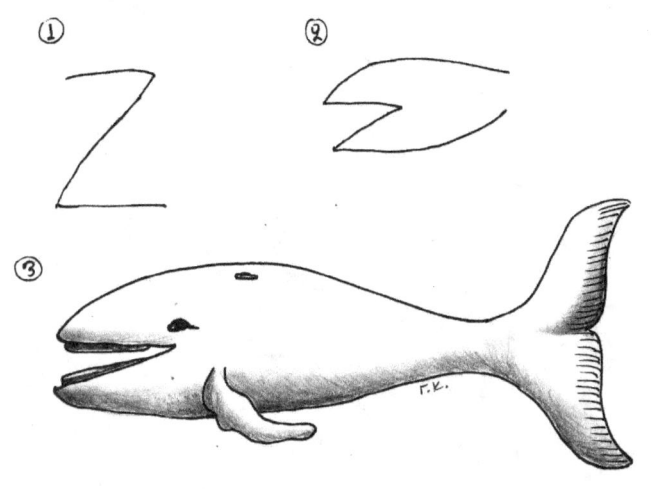

① ② ③

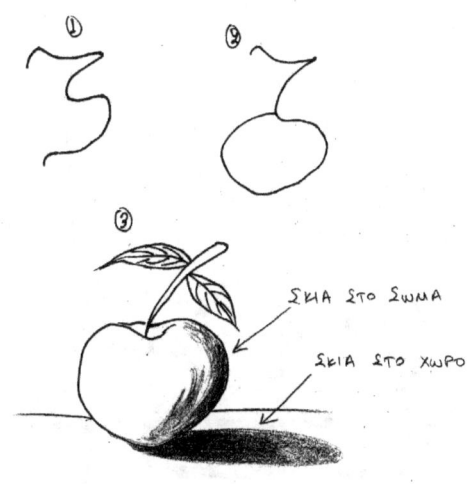

① ② ③

ΣΚΙΑ ΣΤΟ ΣΩΜΑ

ΣΚΙΑ ΣΤΟ ΧΩΡΟ

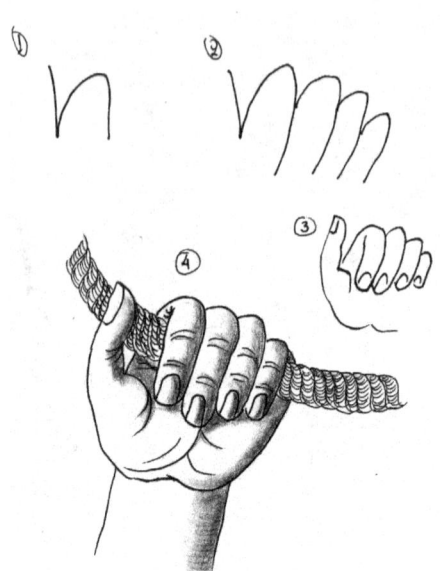

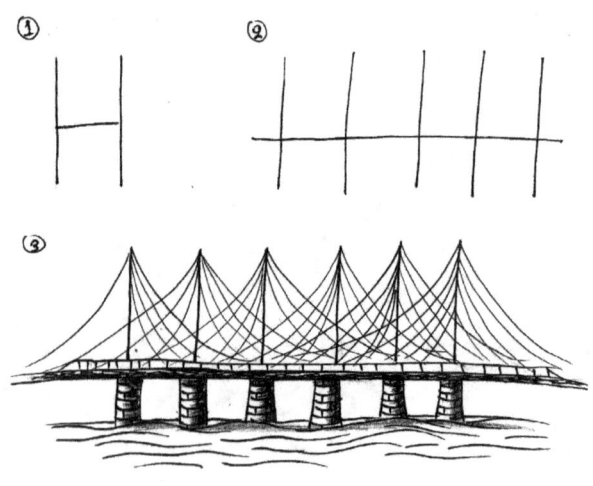

14

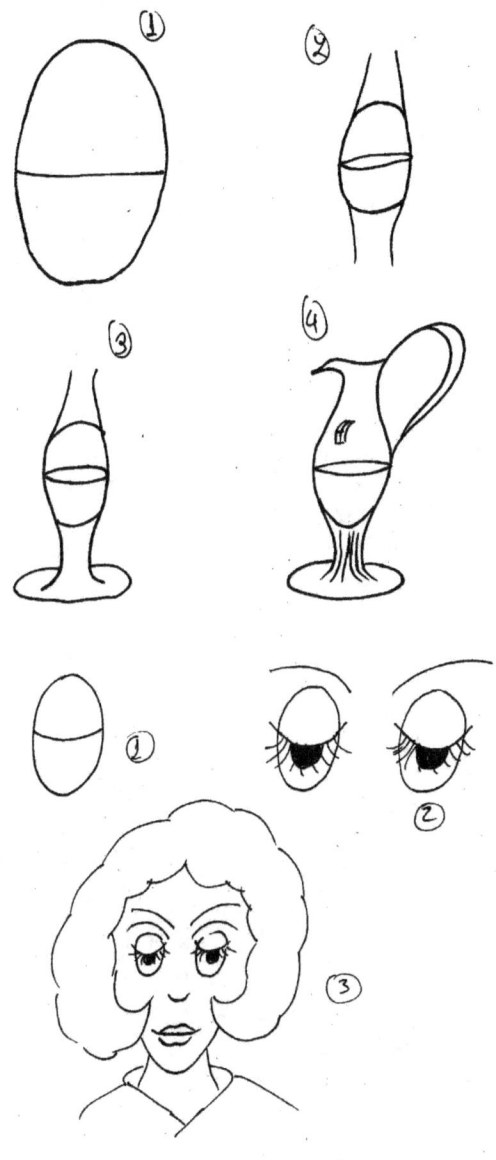

15

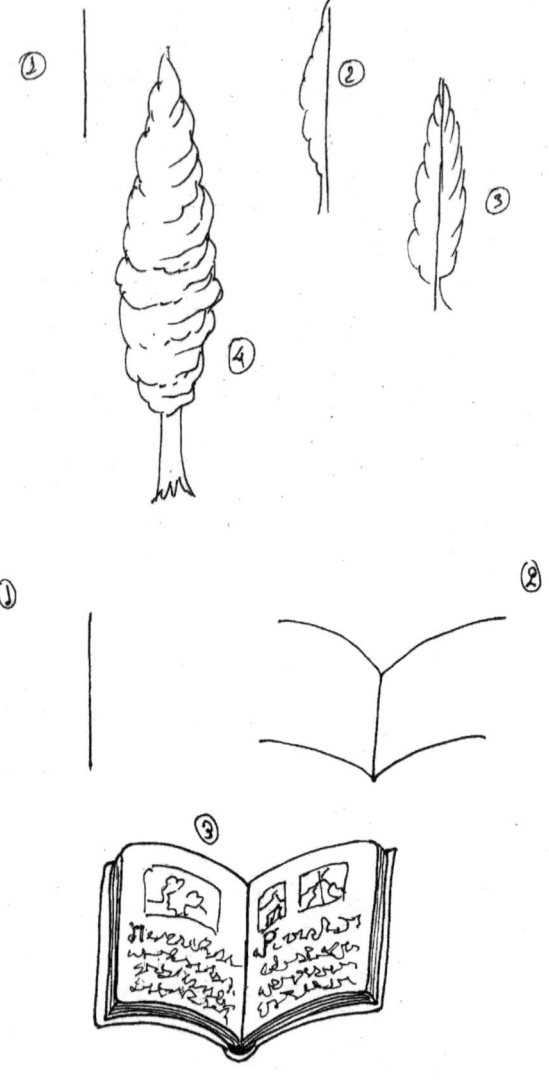

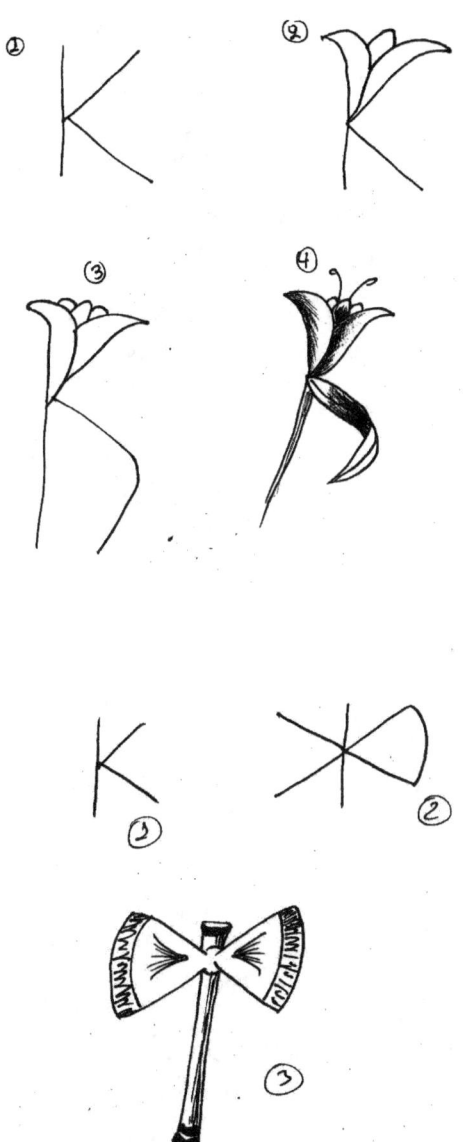

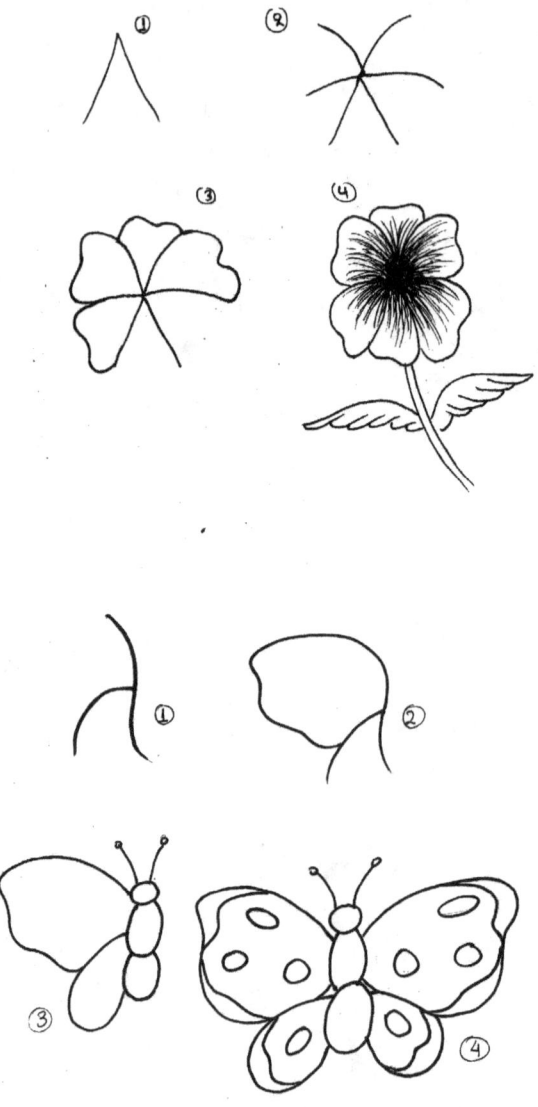

18

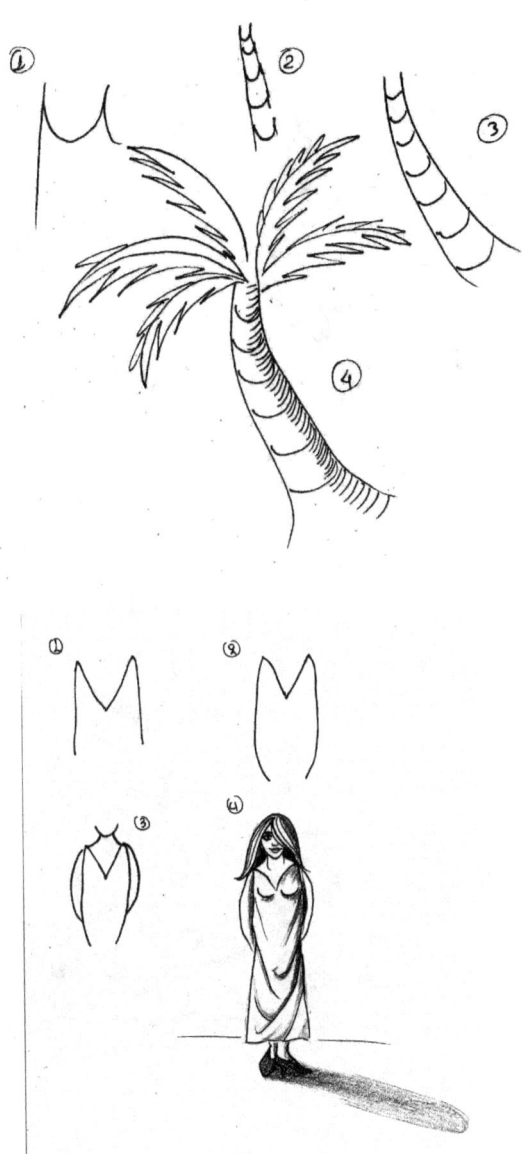

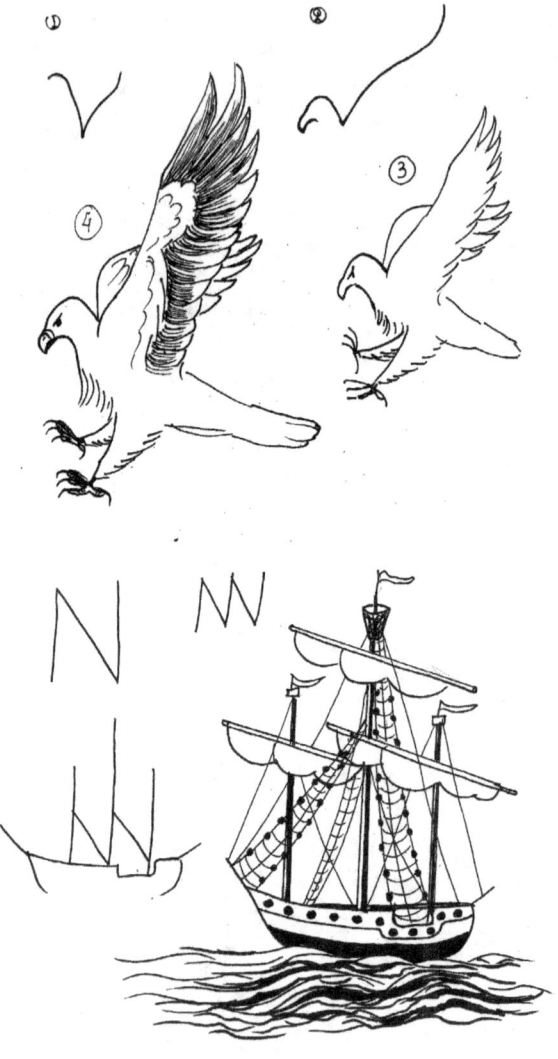

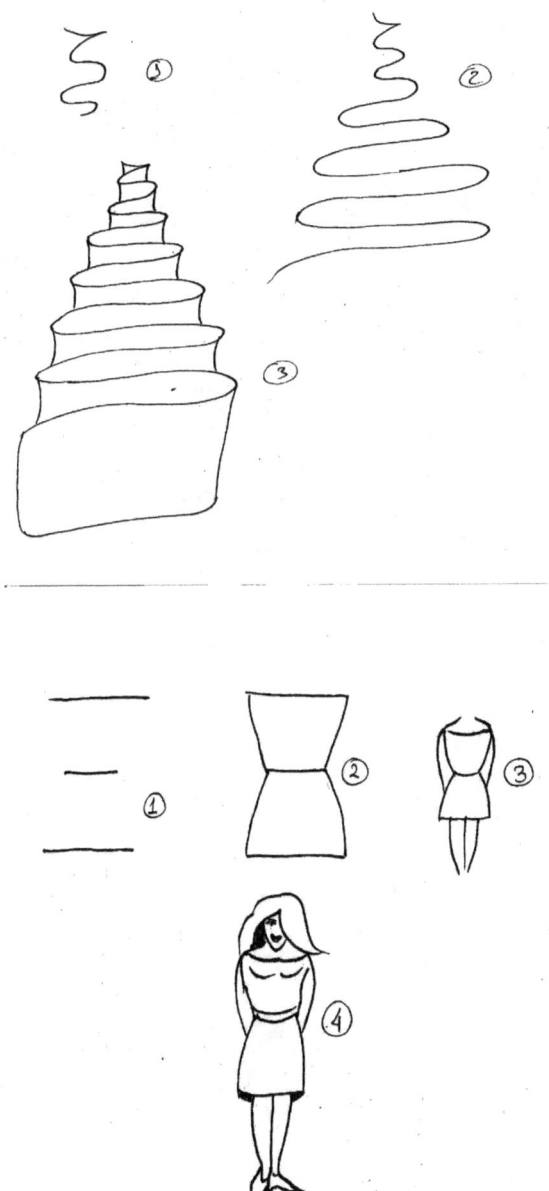

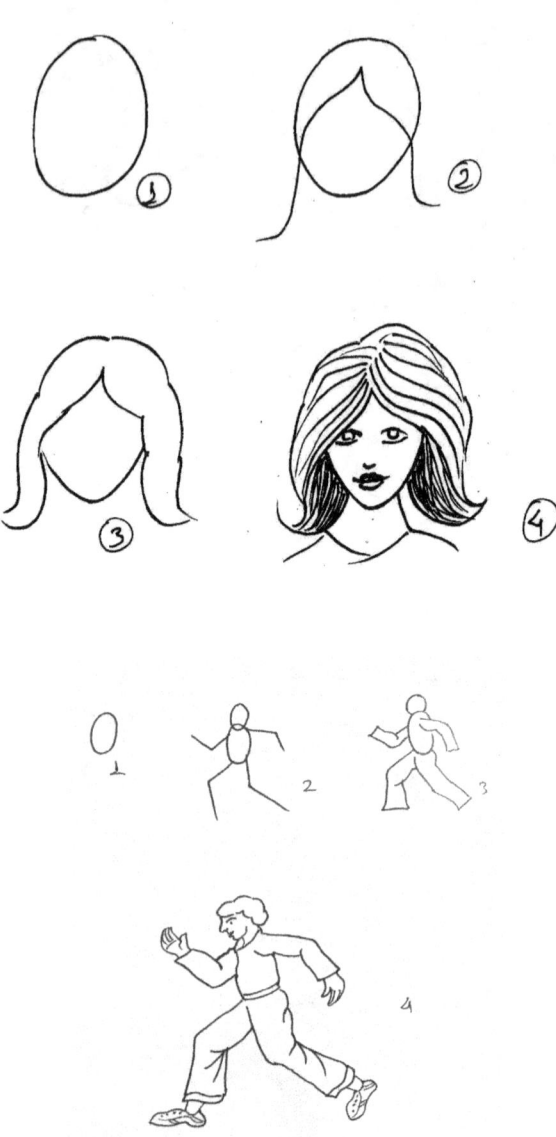

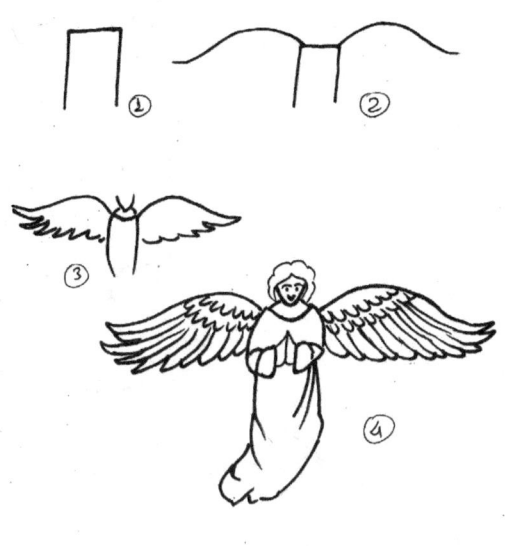

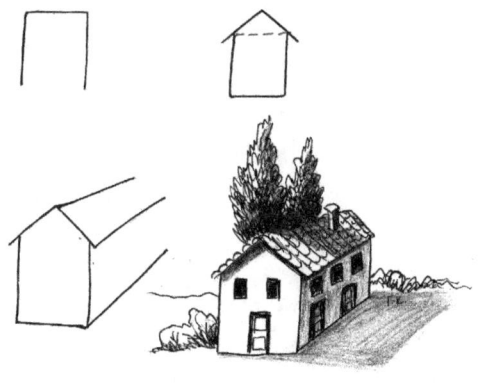

23

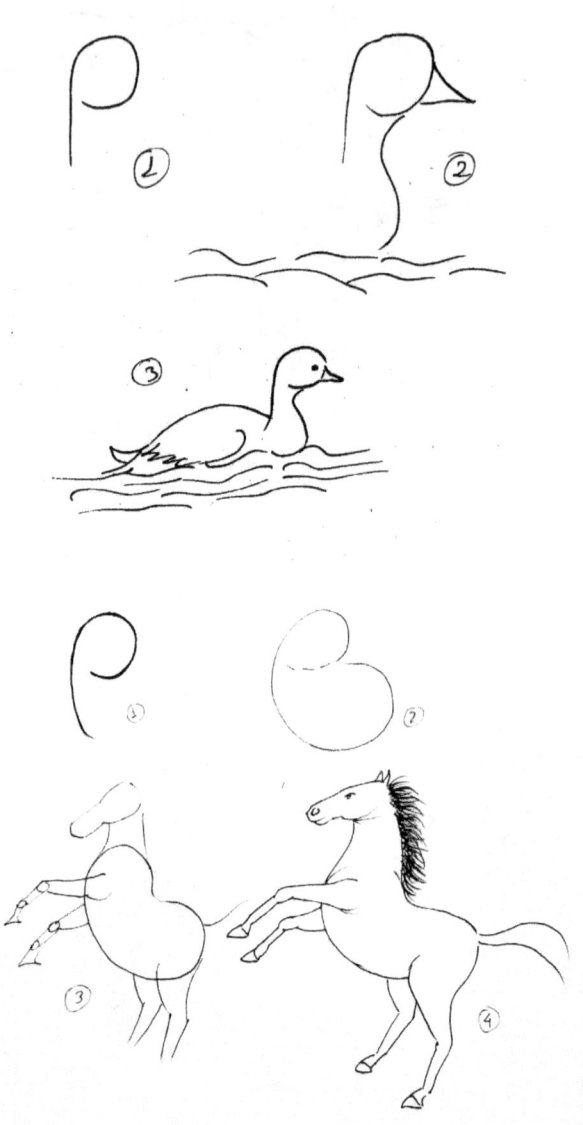

24

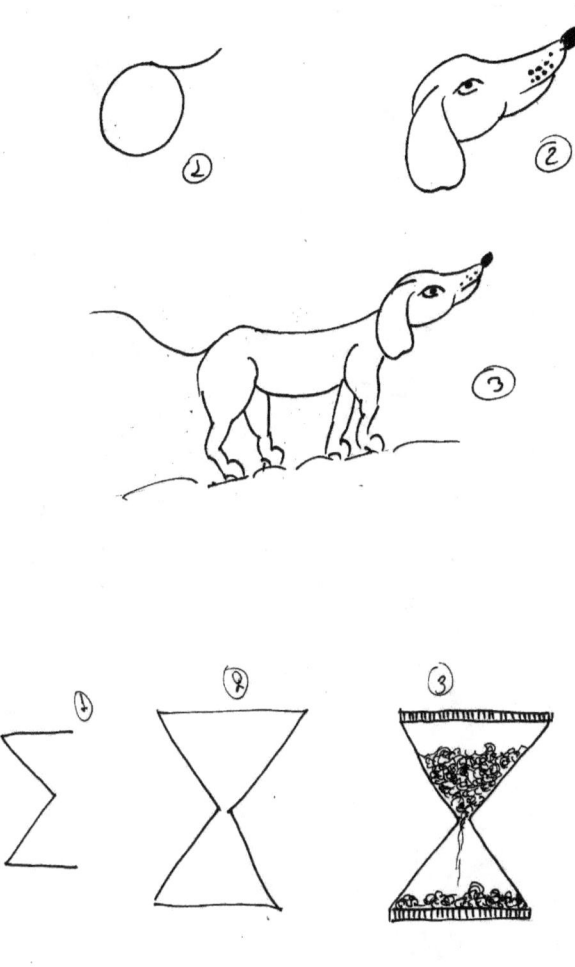

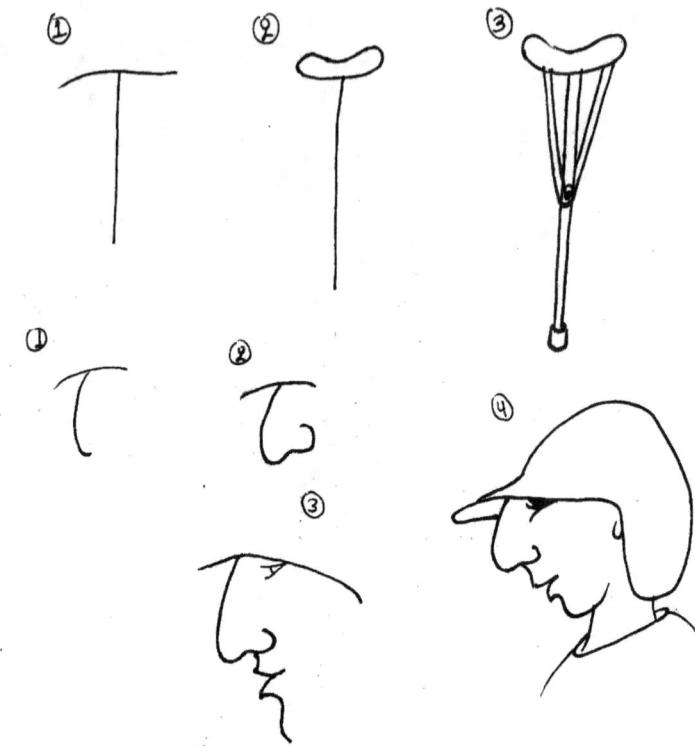

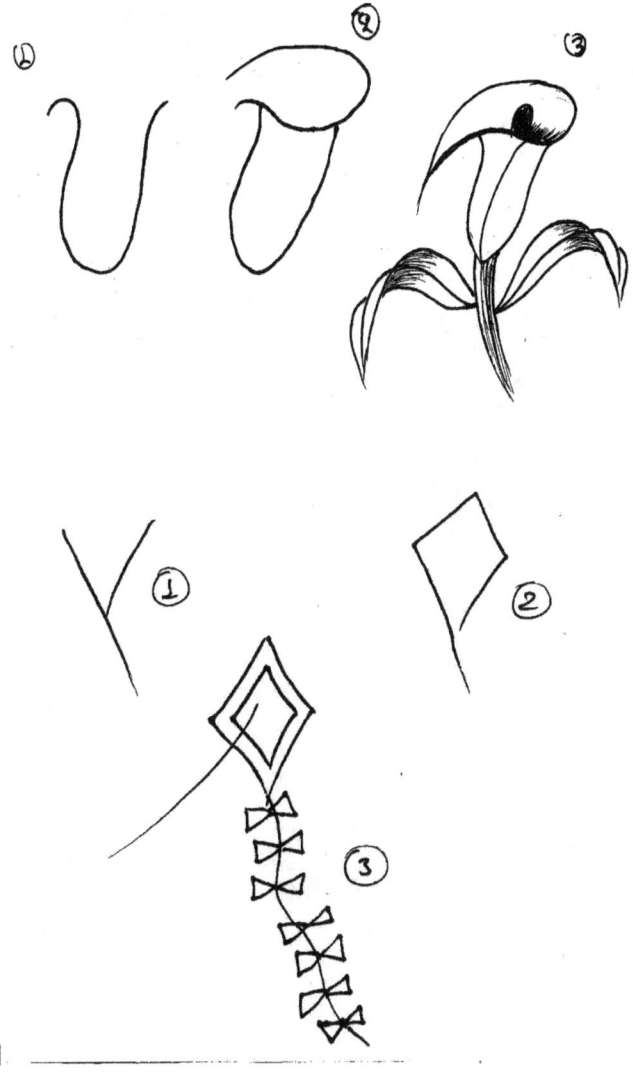

27

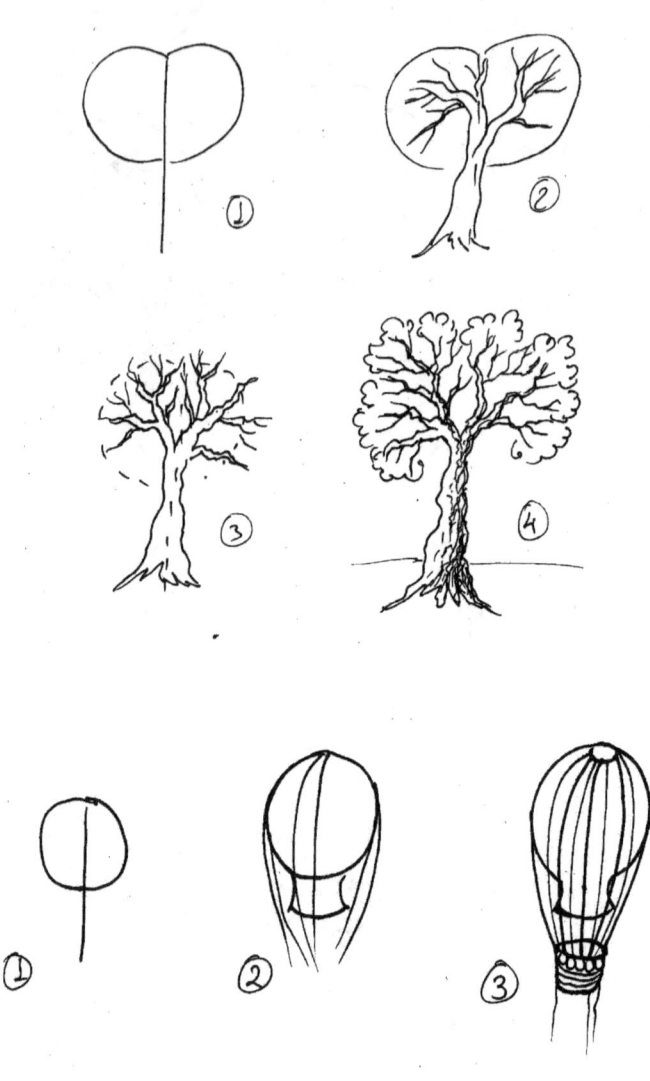

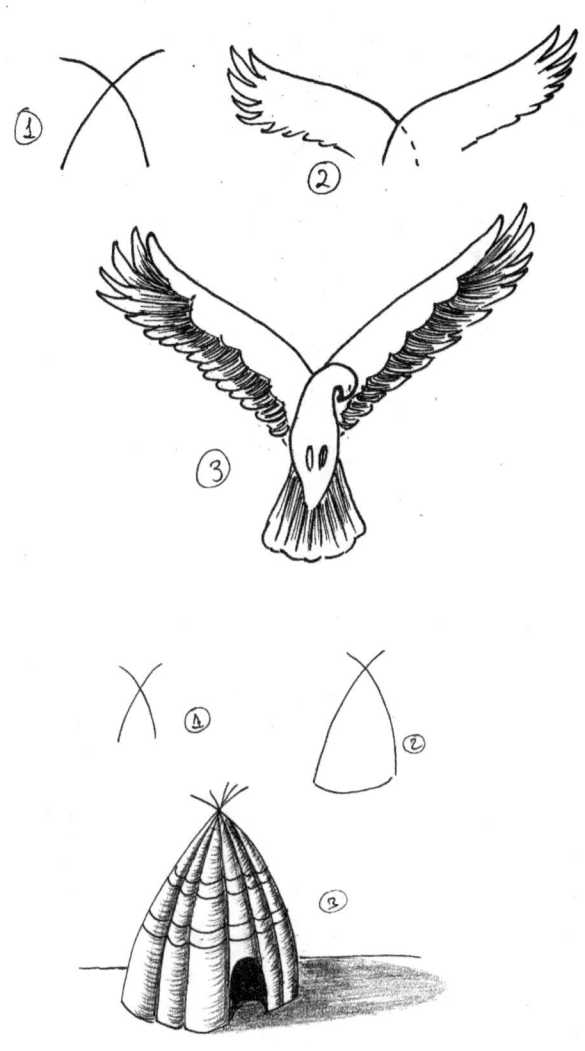

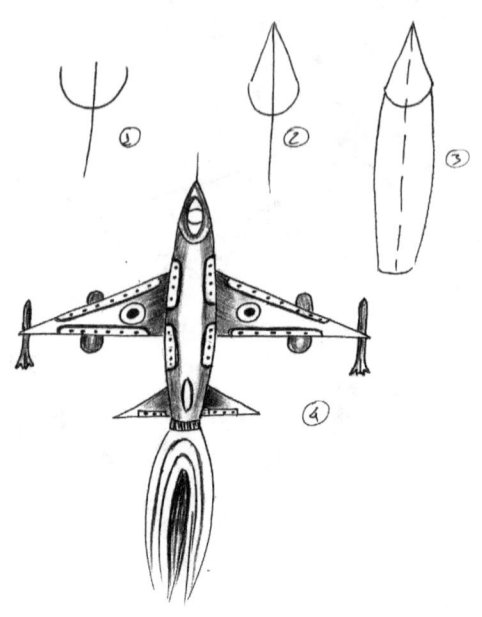

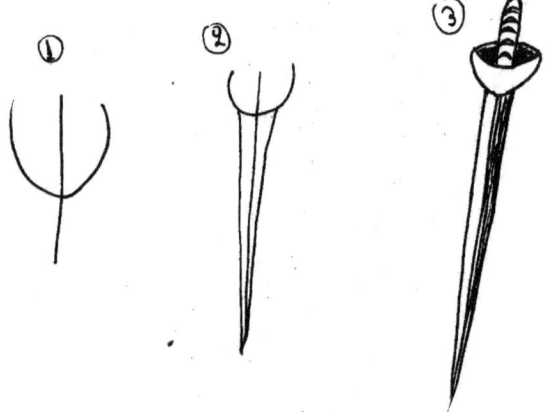

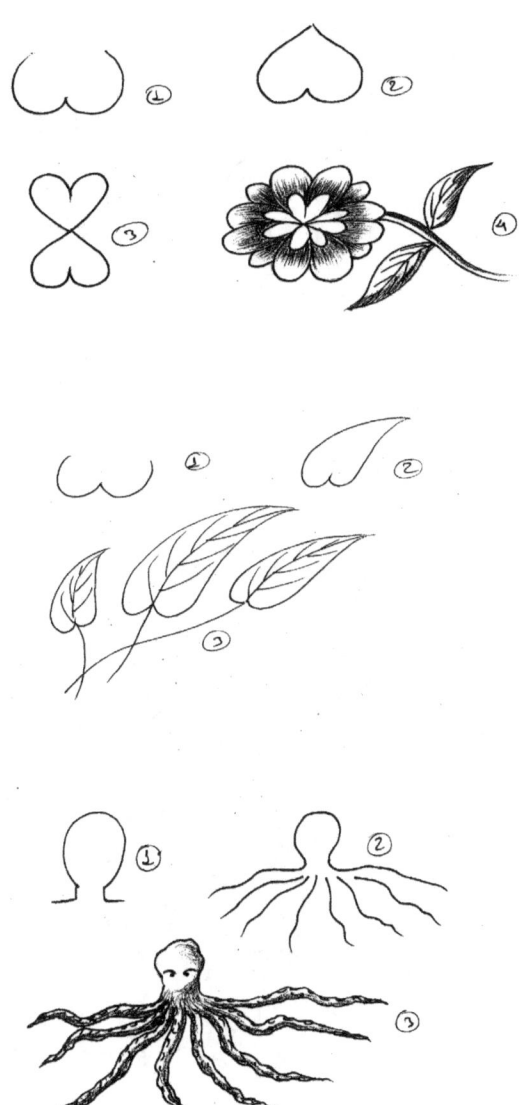

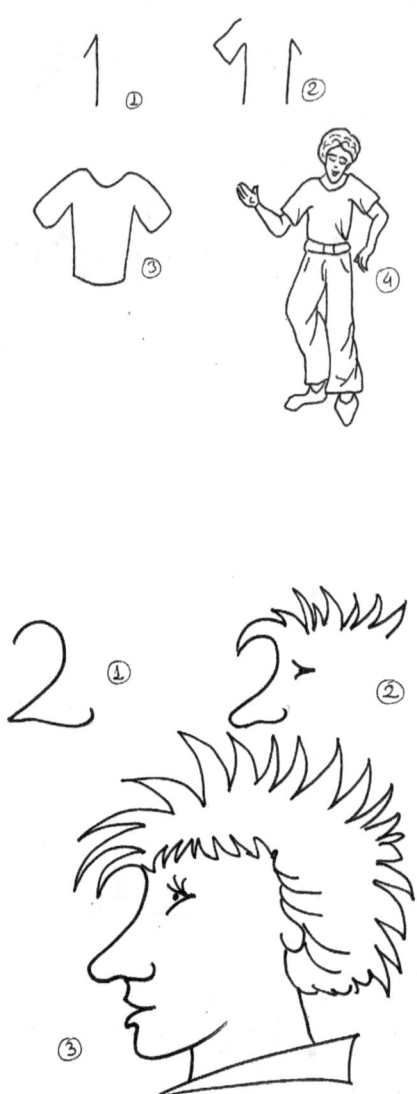

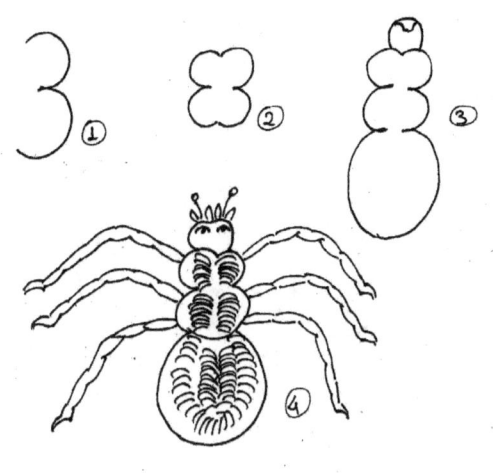

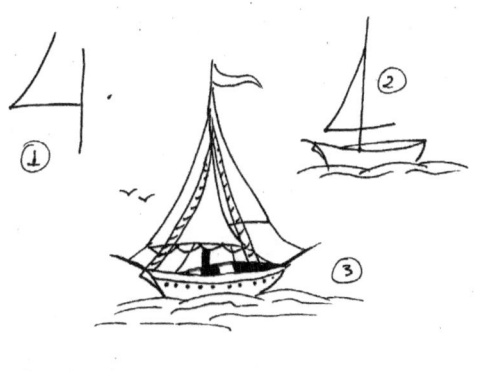

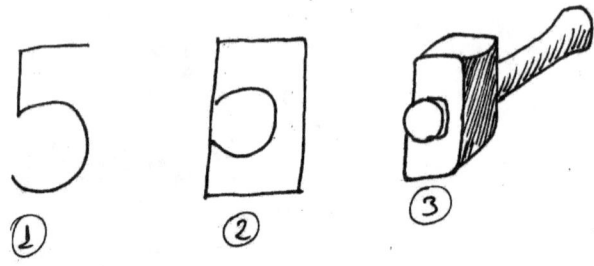

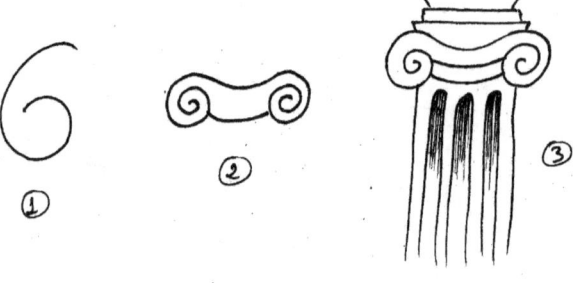

34

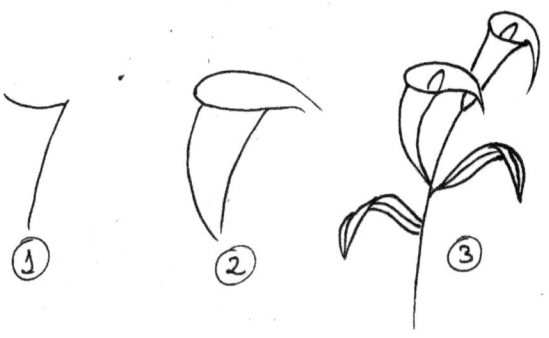

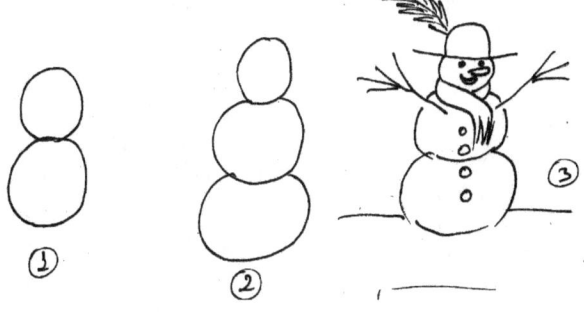

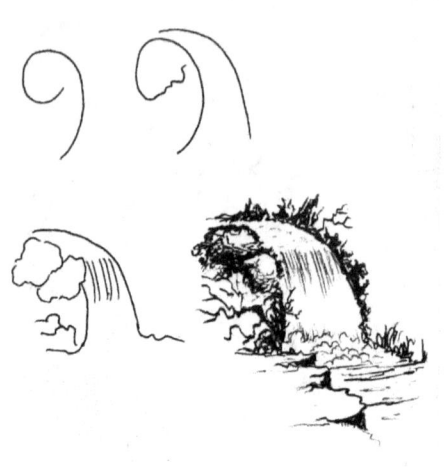

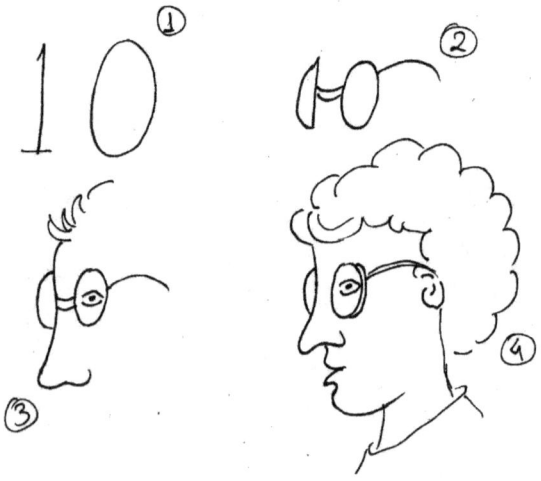

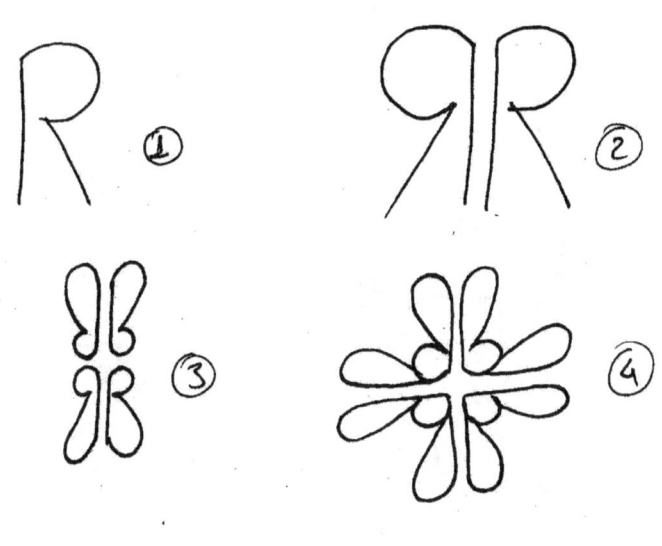

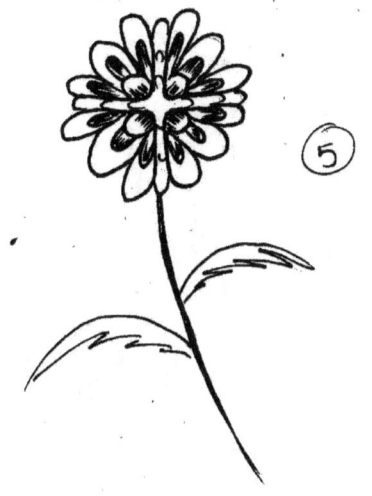

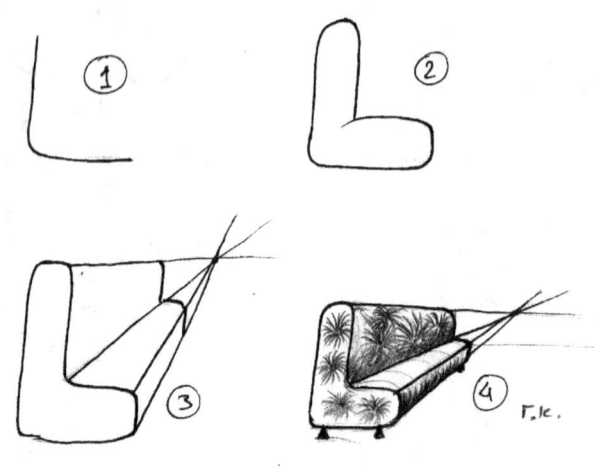

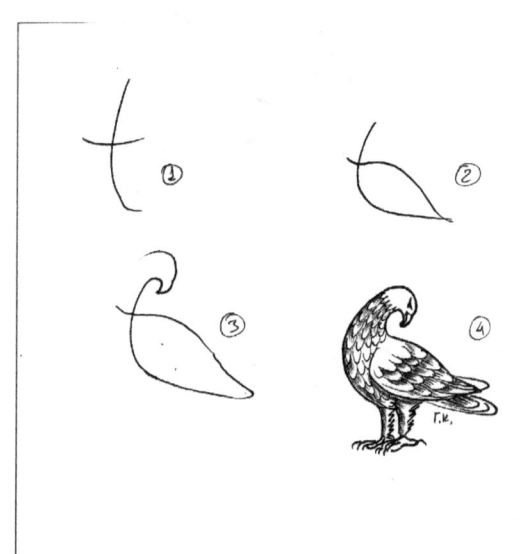

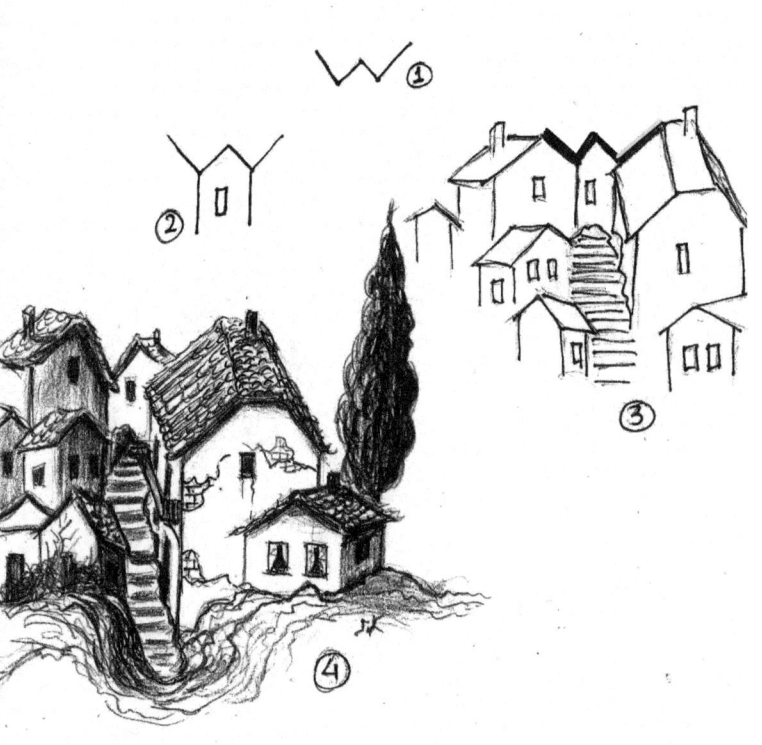

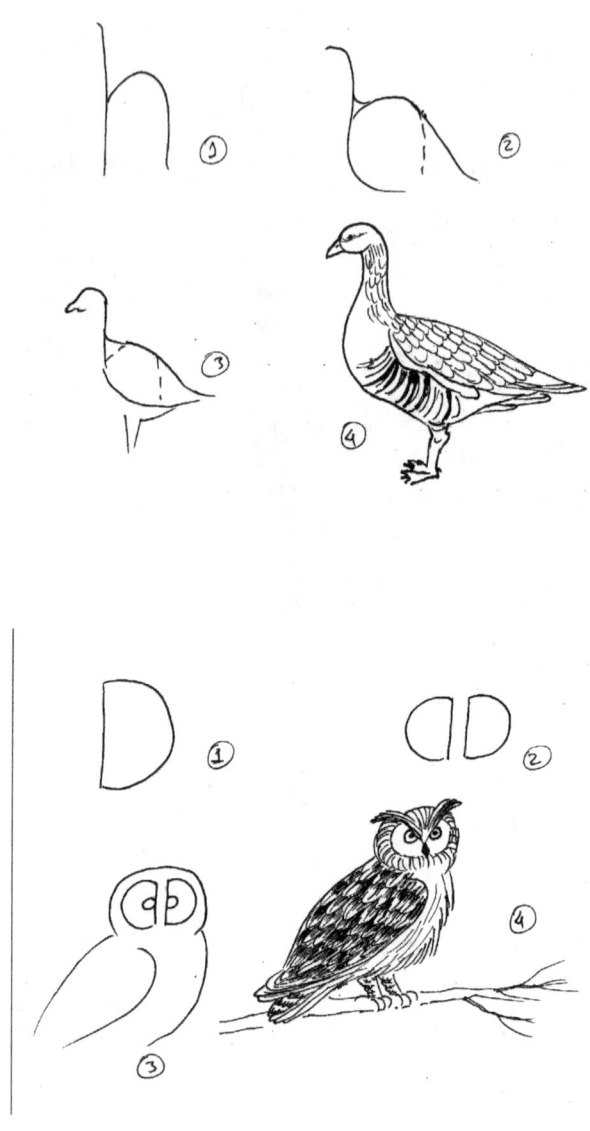

① ② ③ ④

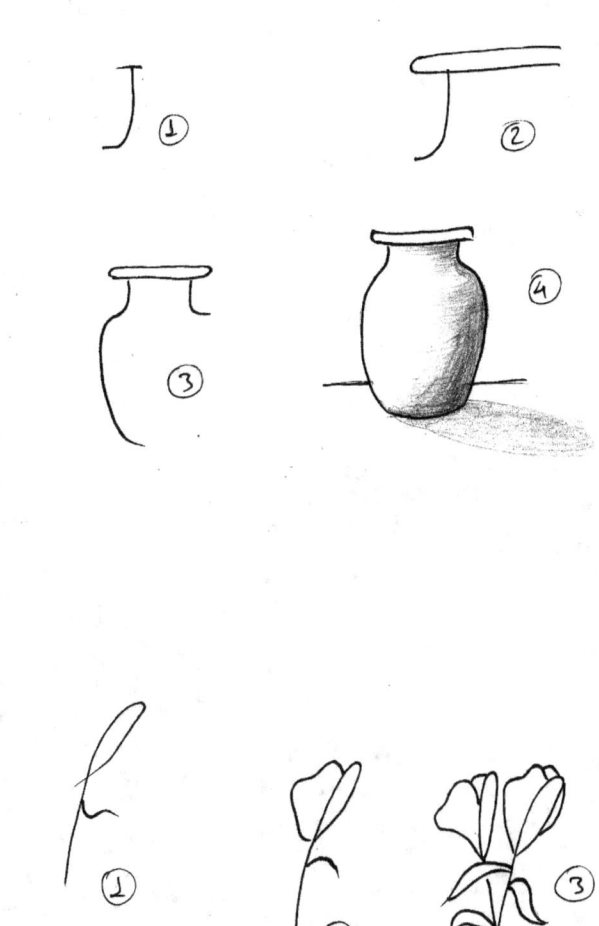

Exercises with drawings of mountains and rocks

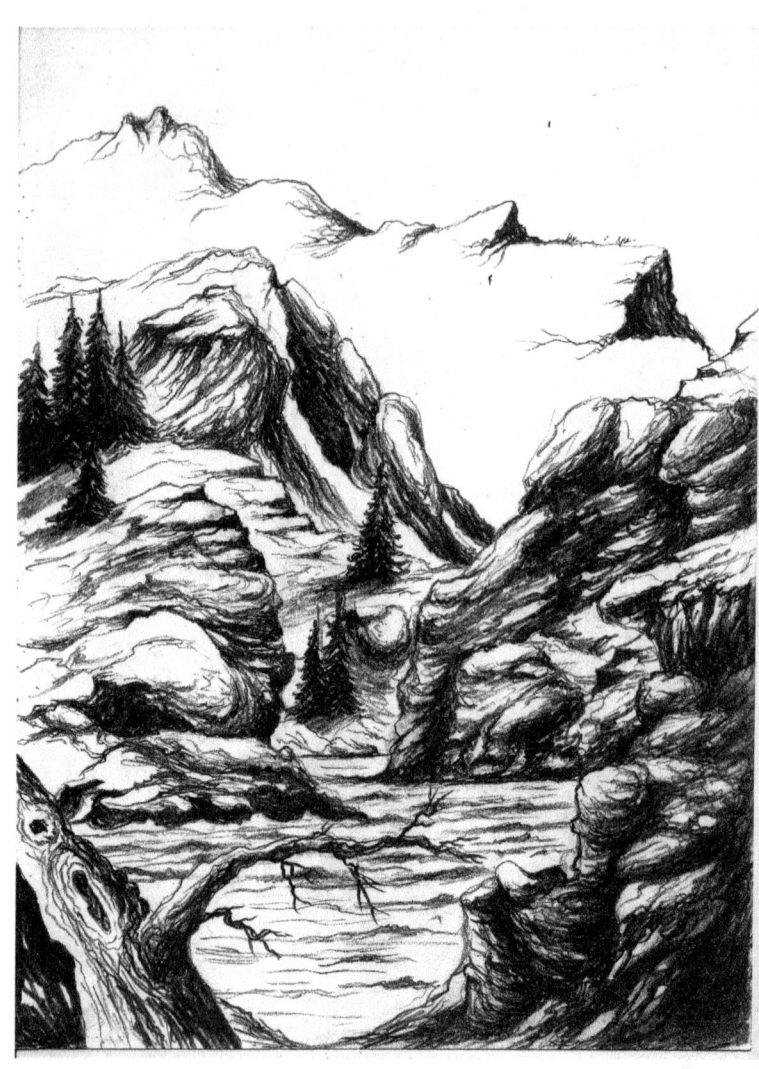

Exercises with fabric patterns

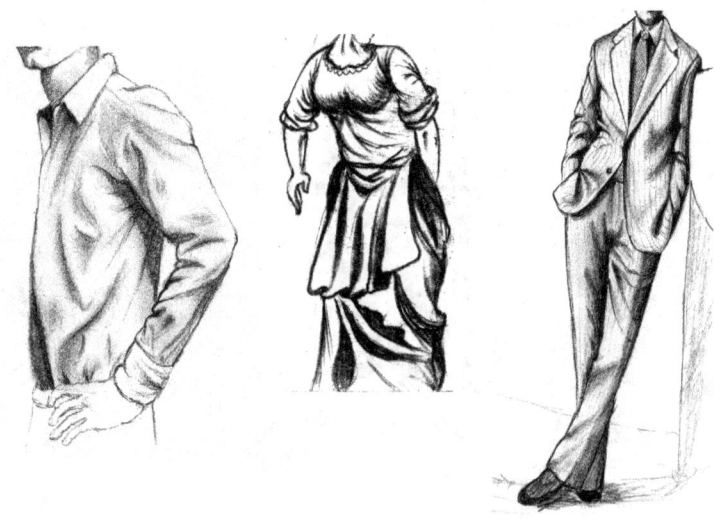

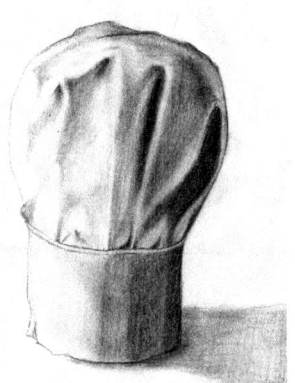

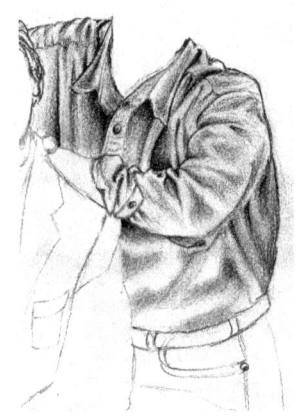

Exercises with sea patterns

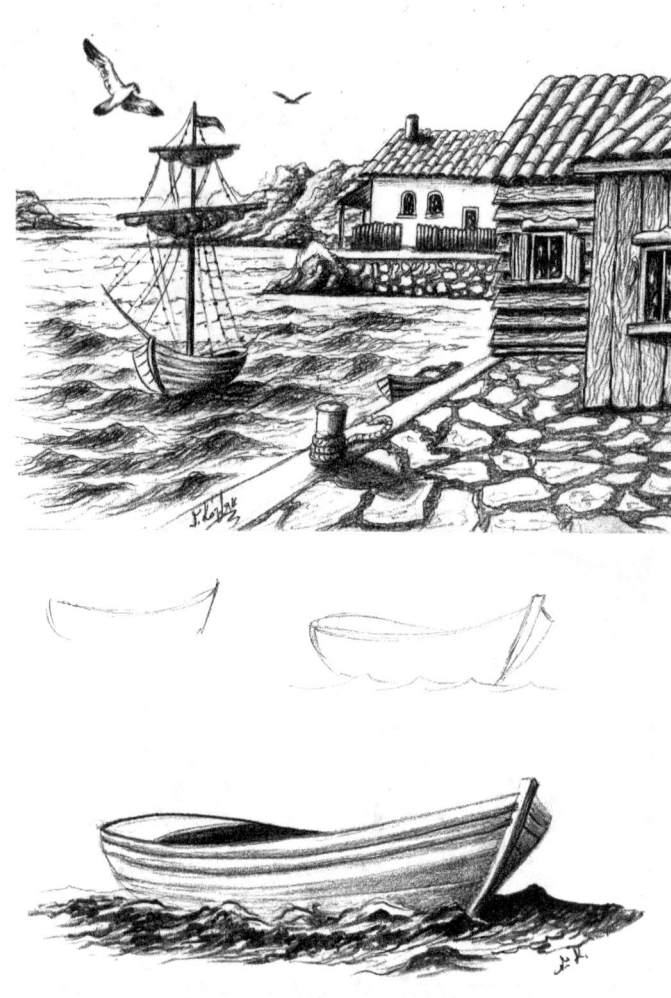

Exercises with sea patterns

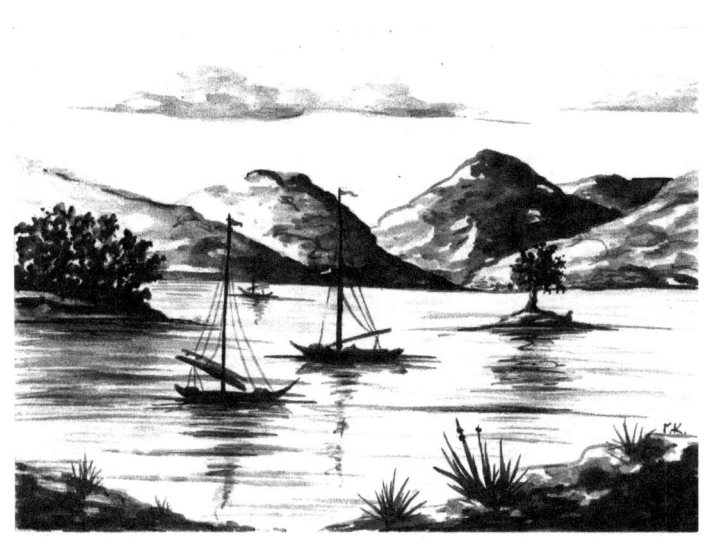

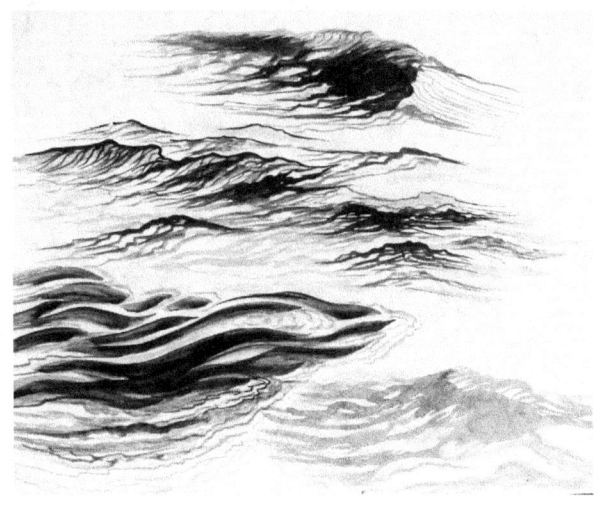

Exercises with hand drawings

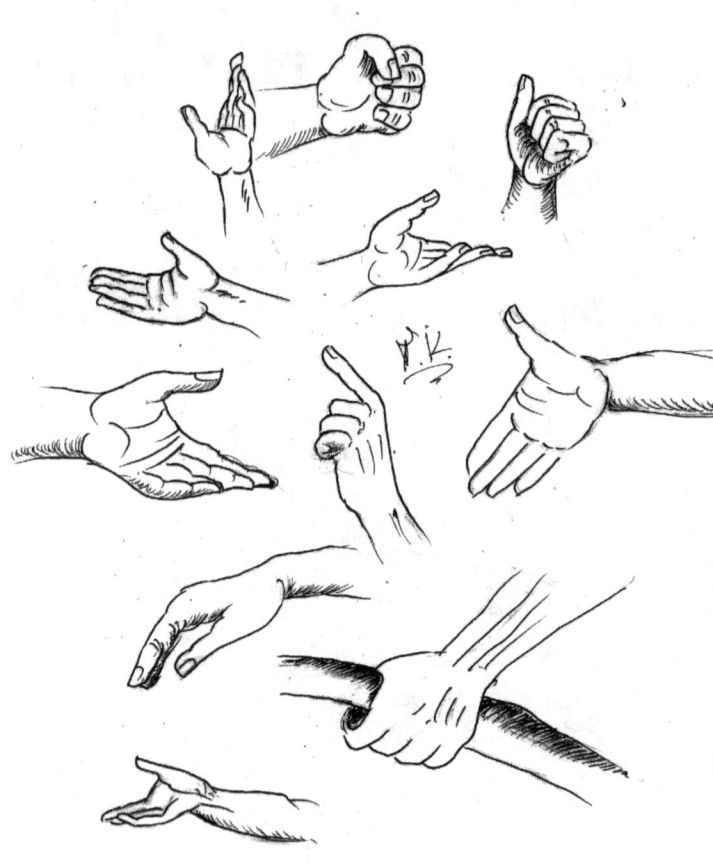

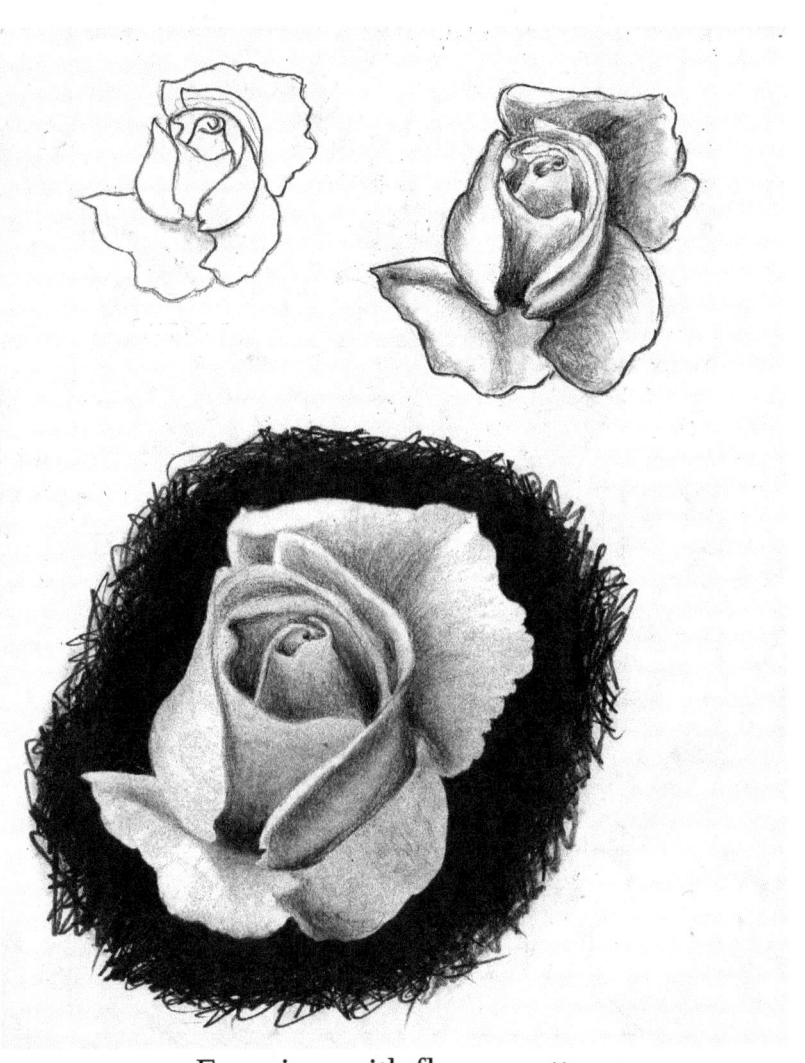

Exercises with flower patterns

Exercises with Perspective drawings

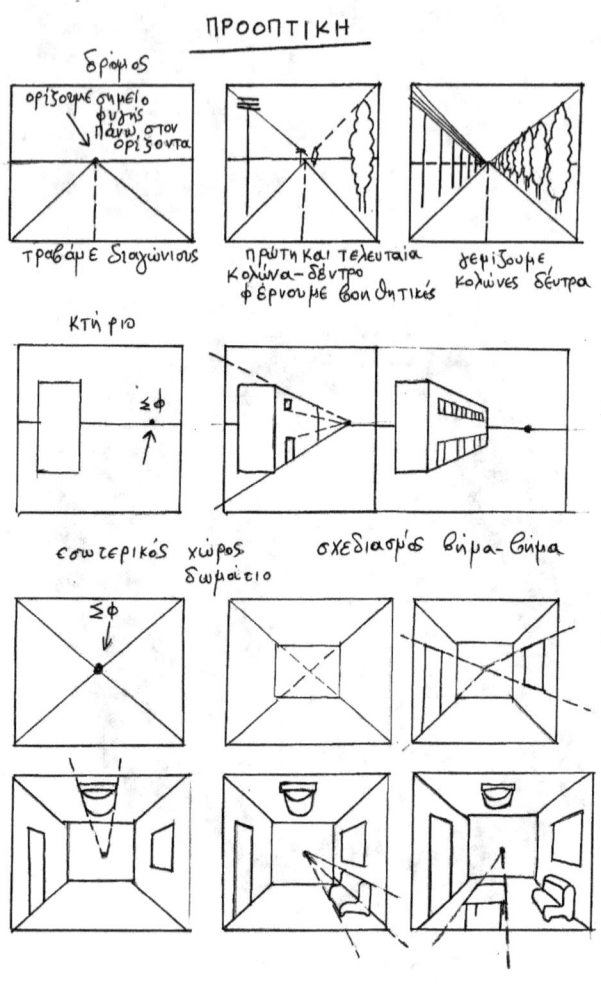

ΠΡΟΟΠΤΙΚΗ

δρόμος

ορίζουμε σημείο
φυγής
πάνω, στον
ορίζοντα

τραβάμε διαγώνιους

πρώτη και τελευταία
κολώνα-δέντρο
φέρνουμε βοηθητικές

γεμίζουμε
κολώνες δέντρα

κτήριο

Σφ

εσωτερικός χώρος
δωμάτιο

σχεδιασμός βήμα-βήμα

Σφ

Exercises with Perspective drawings

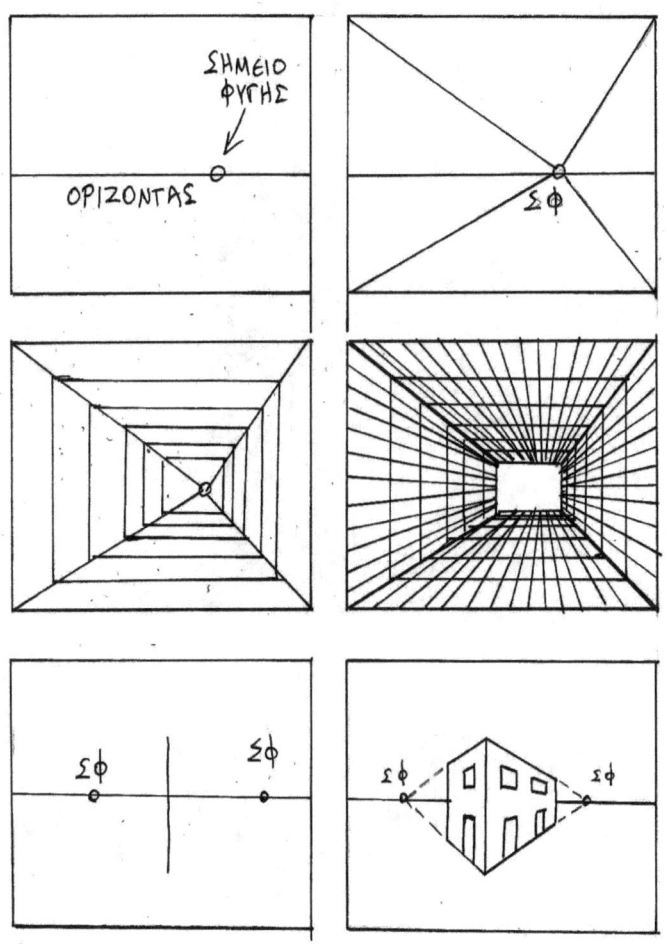

Exercises with Perspective drawings

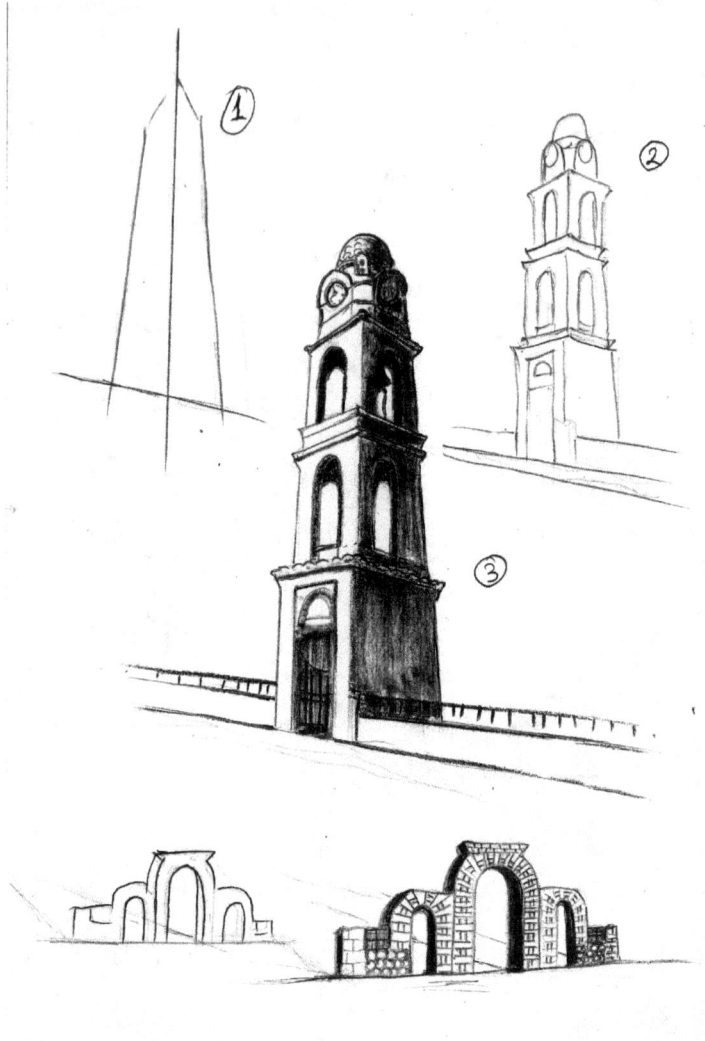

Exercises with Perspective drawings

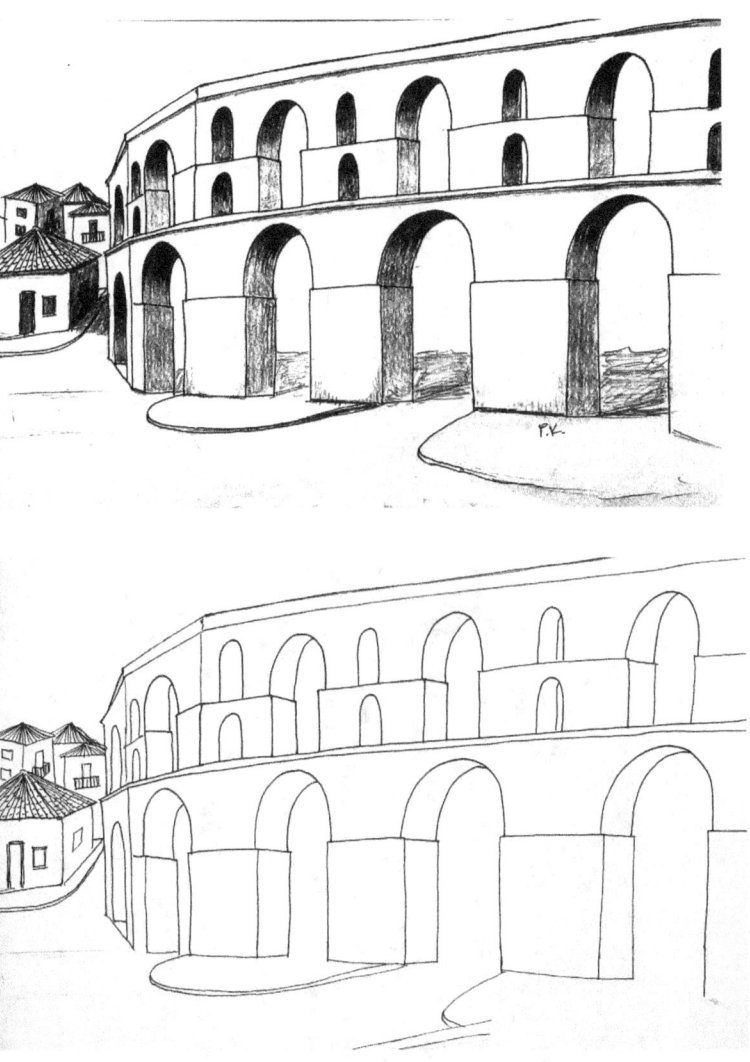

Exercises with Perspective drawings

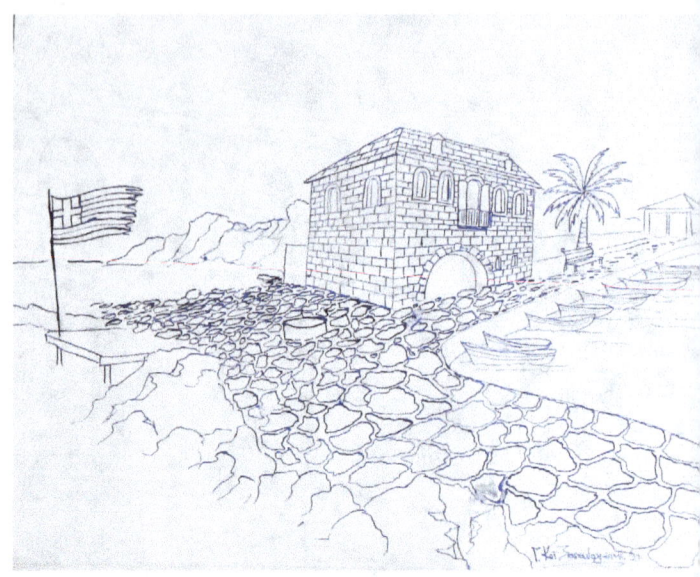

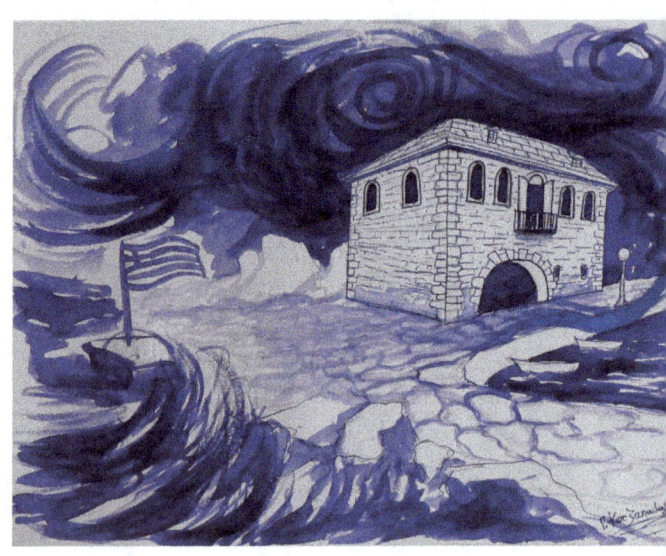

Exercises with Perspective drawings

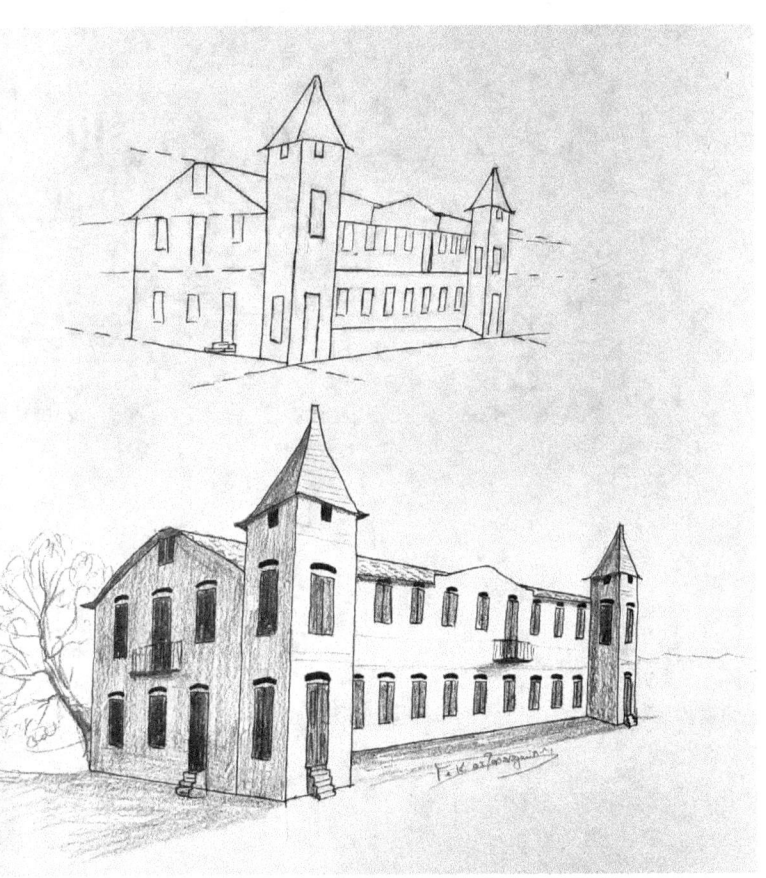

Exercises with Perspective drawings

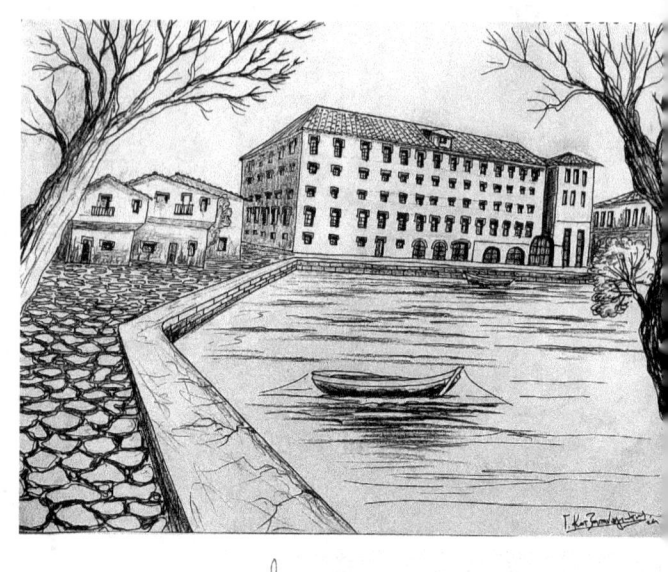

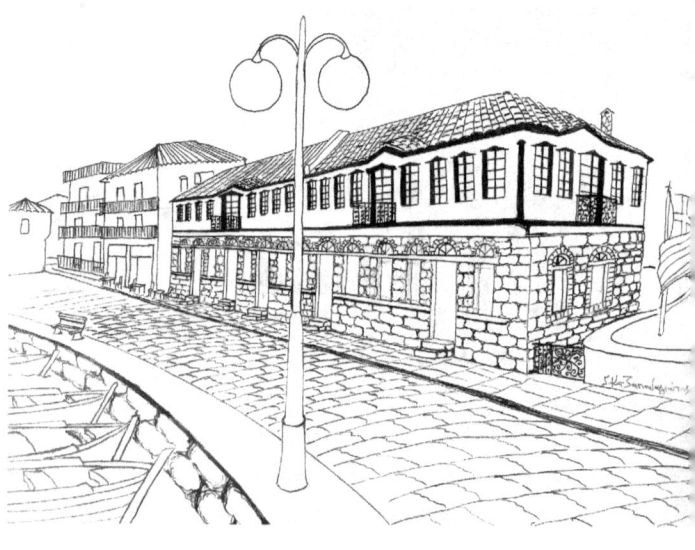

Drawing brushes for painting

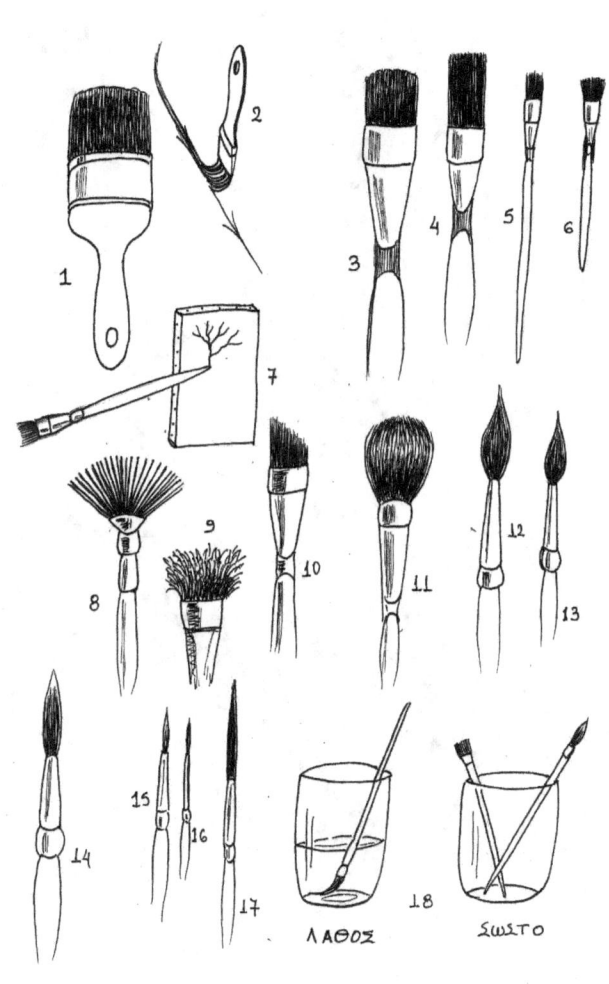

ΛΑΘΟΣ

ΣΩΣΤΟ

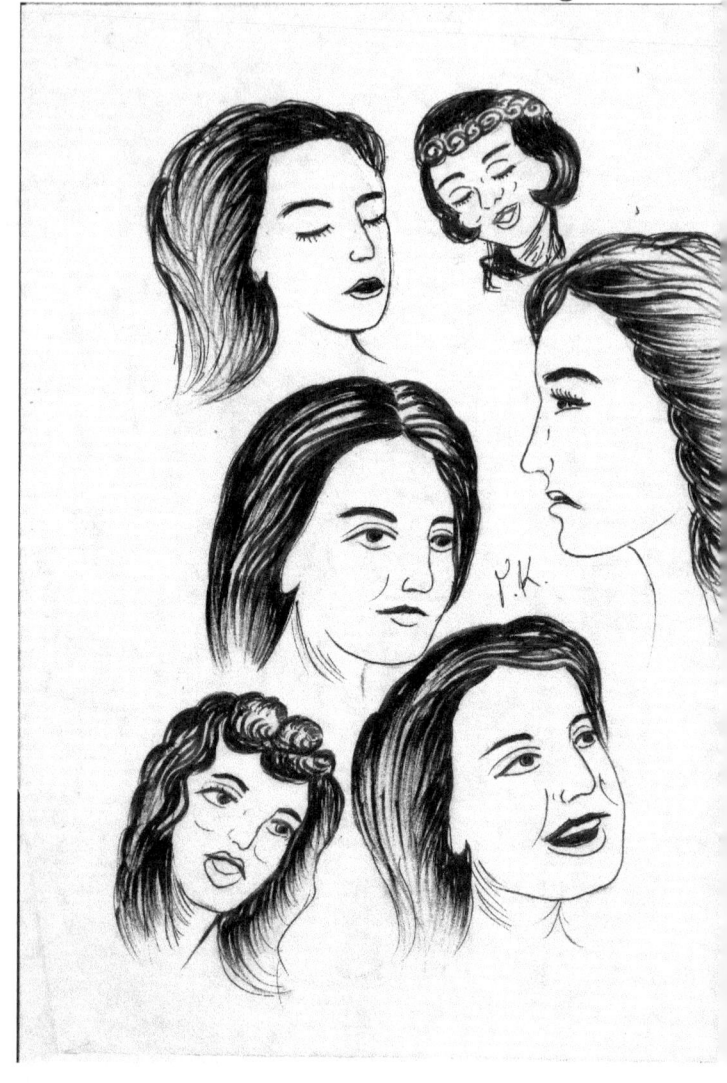

Exercises with face drawings

ΠΡΟΣΩΠΑ

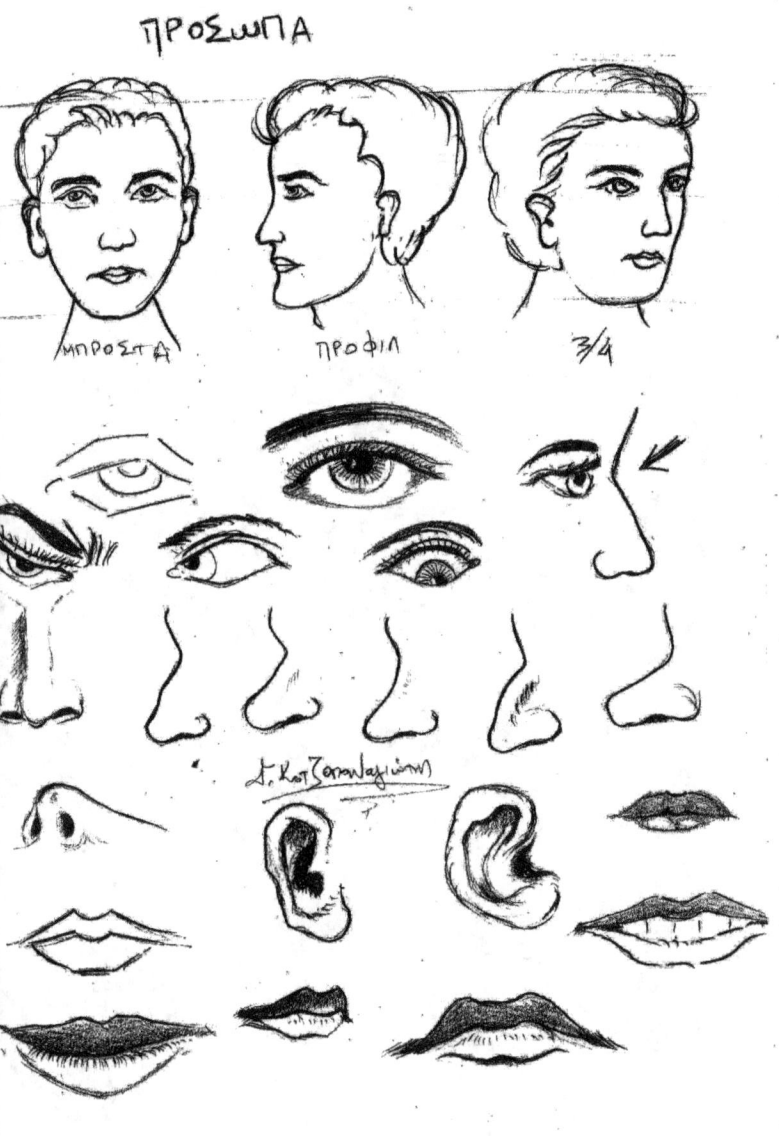

ΜΠΡΟΣΤΑ   ΠΡΟΦΙΛ   3/4

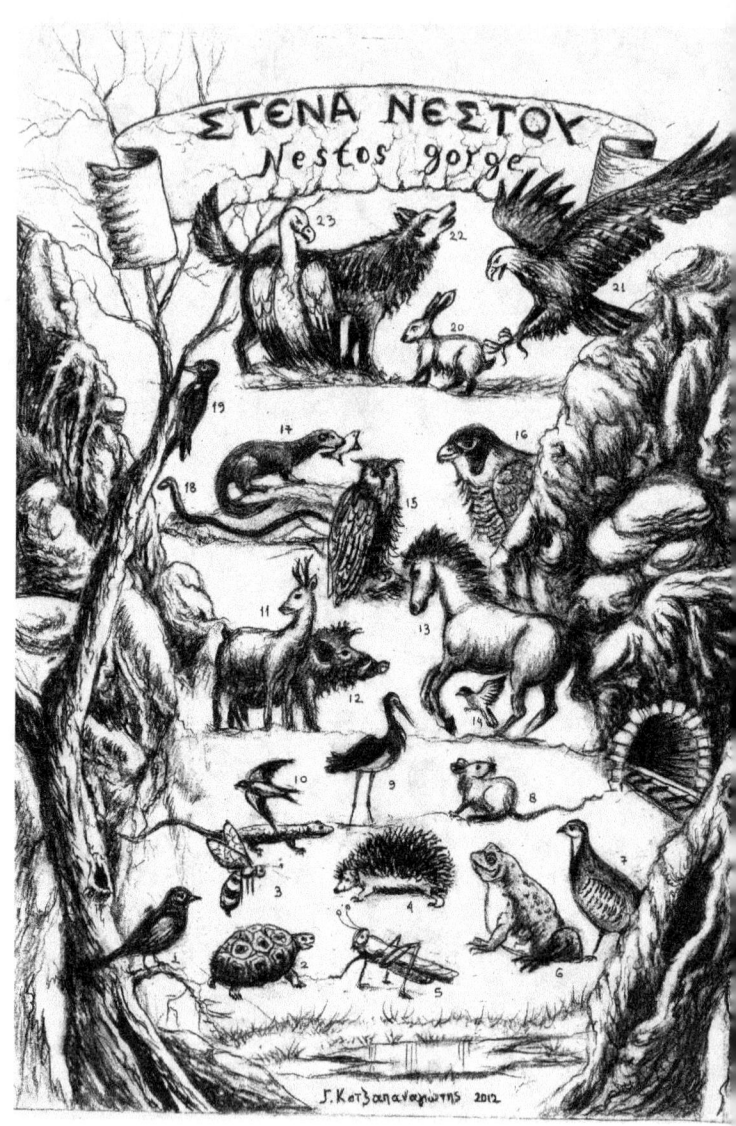

Exercises with animal drawings

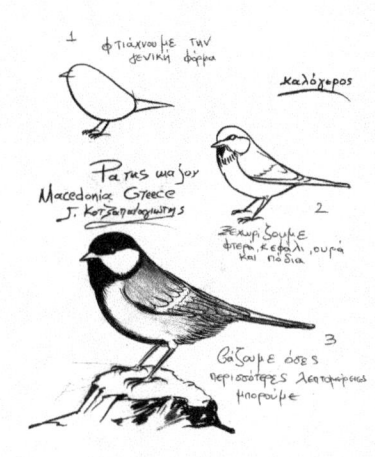

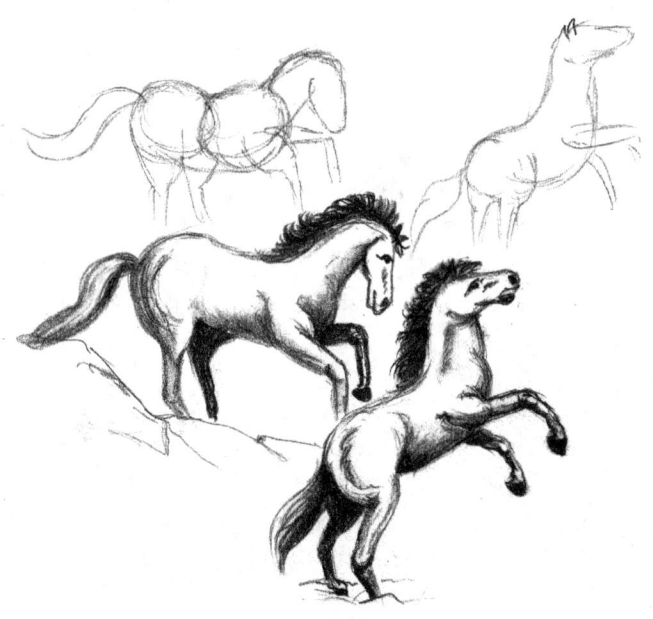

Exercises with flower patterns

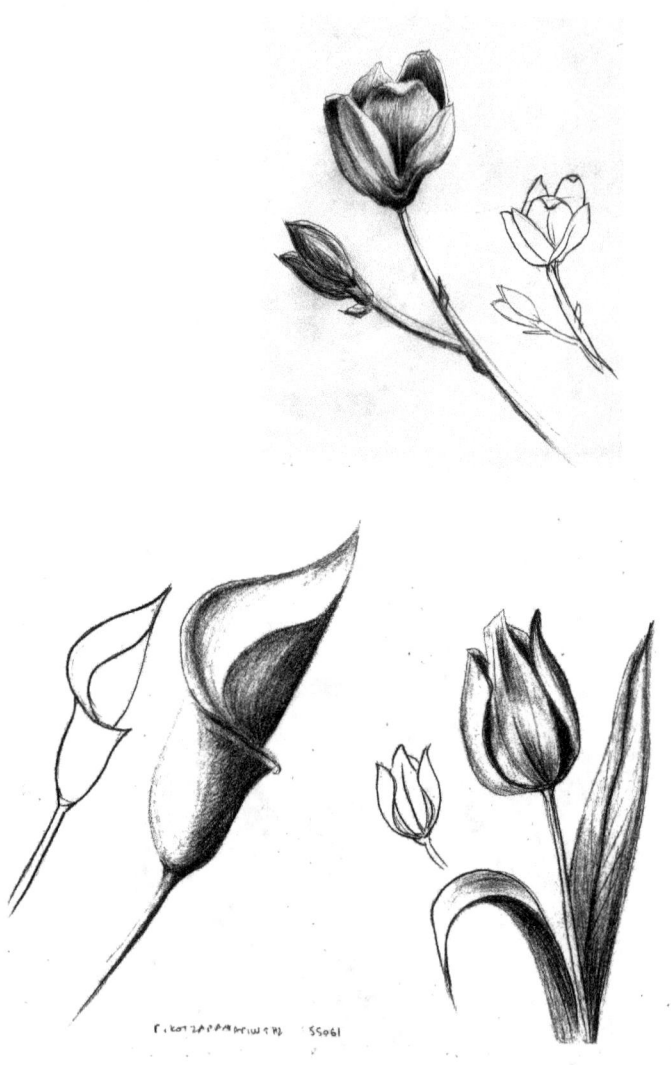

Exercises with animal drawings

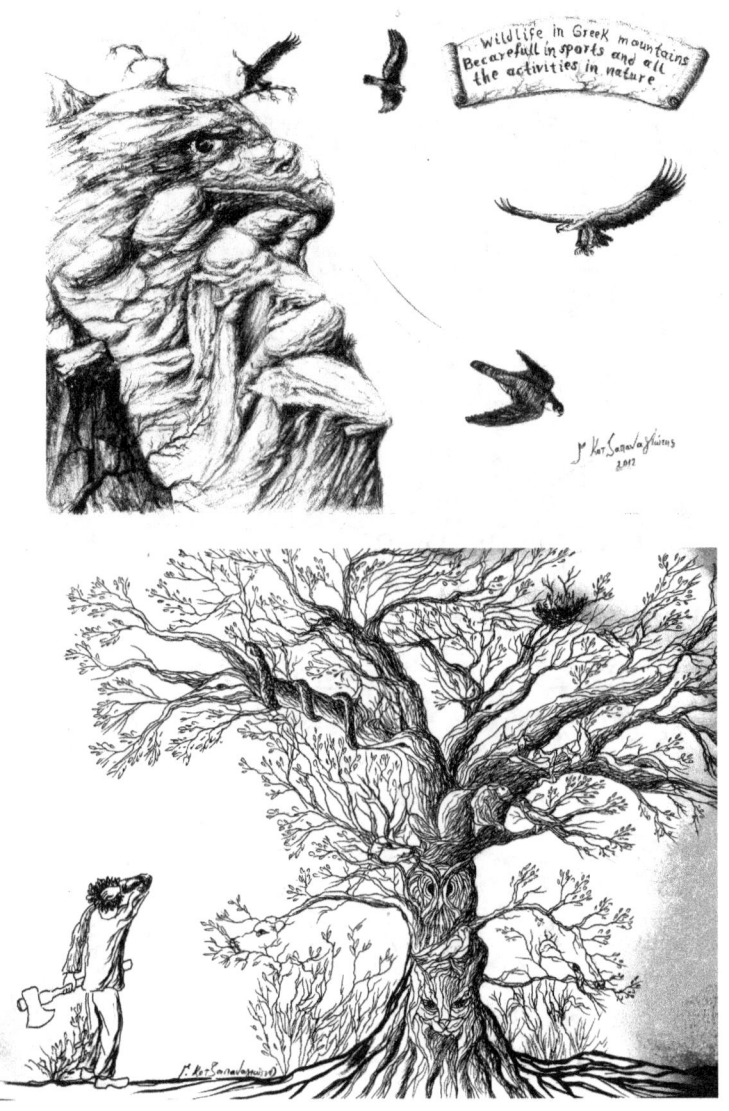

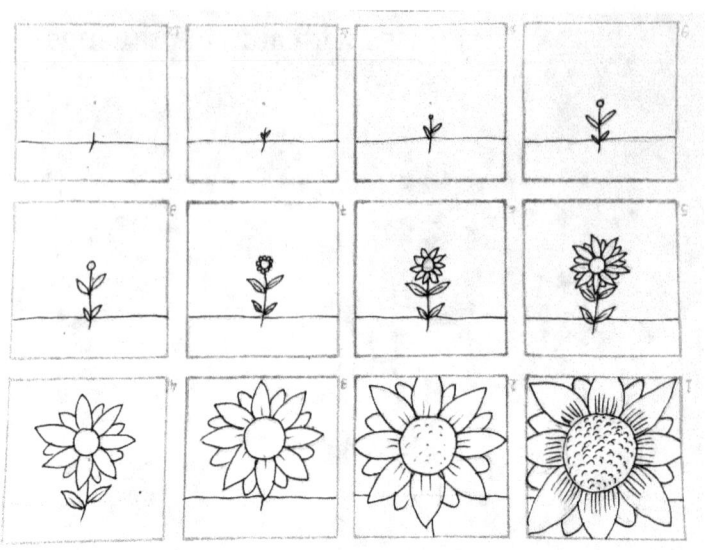

Drawings for cartoons

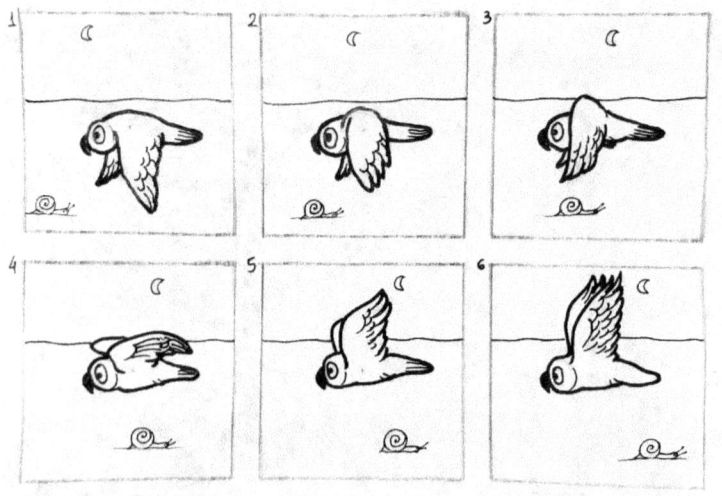

Drawings for cartoons

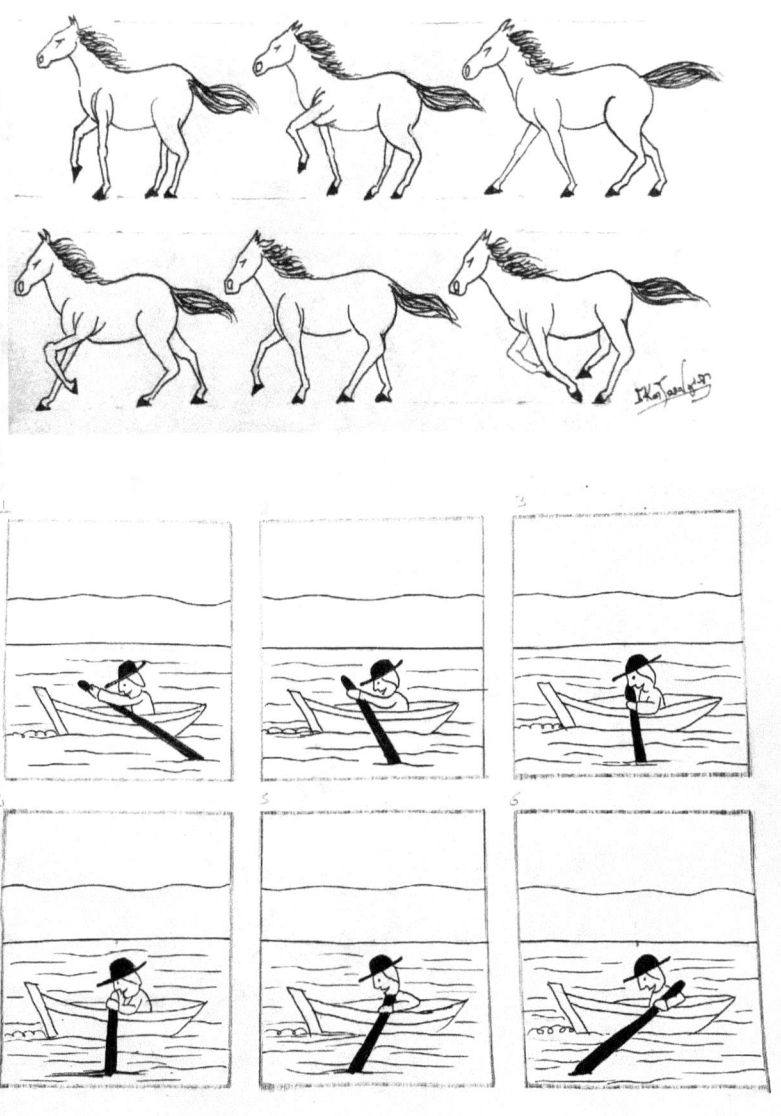

Landscape painting with a palette knife

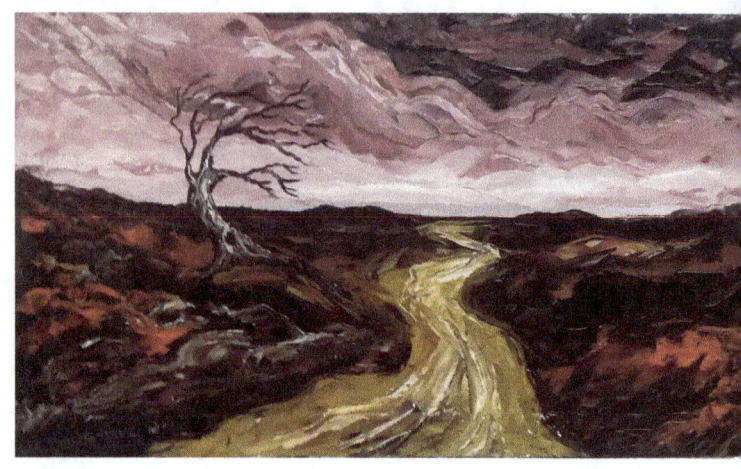

Drawings of wild animals

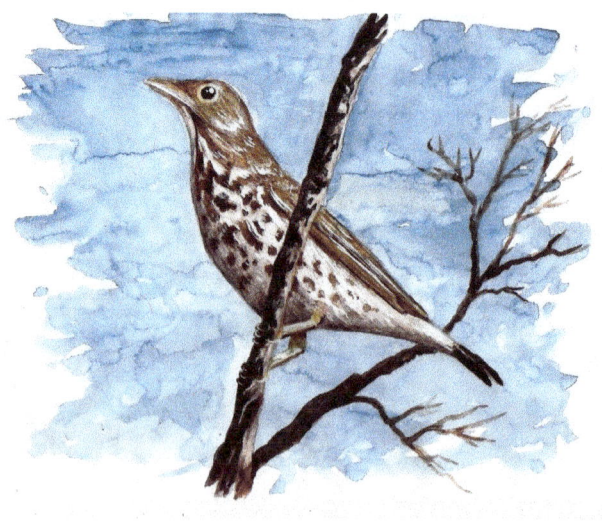

Drawings of wild animals

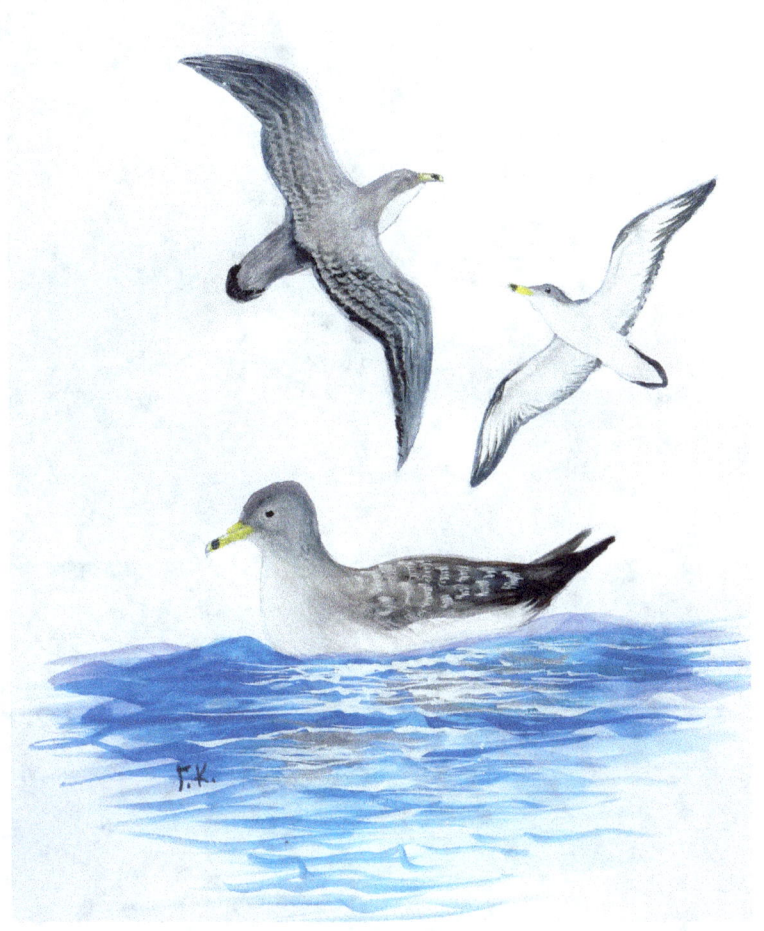

Wild animal painting

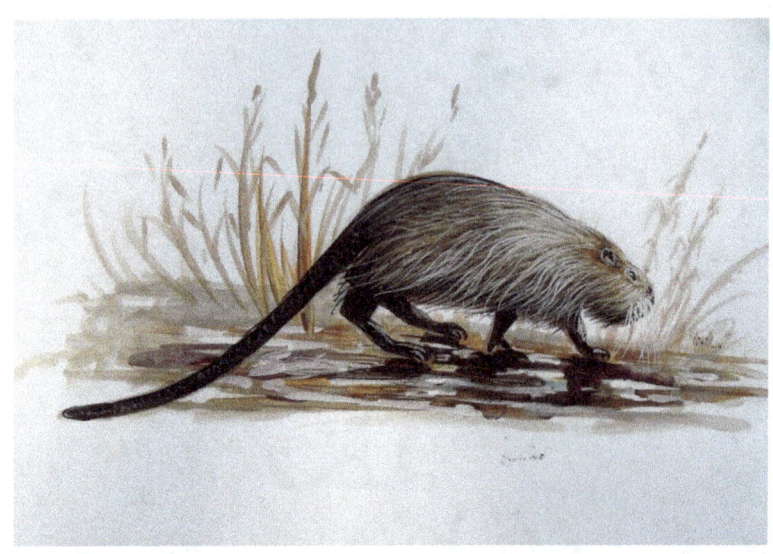

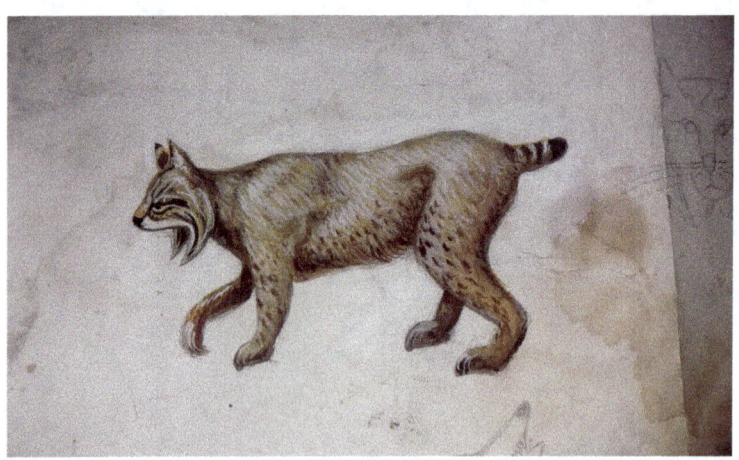

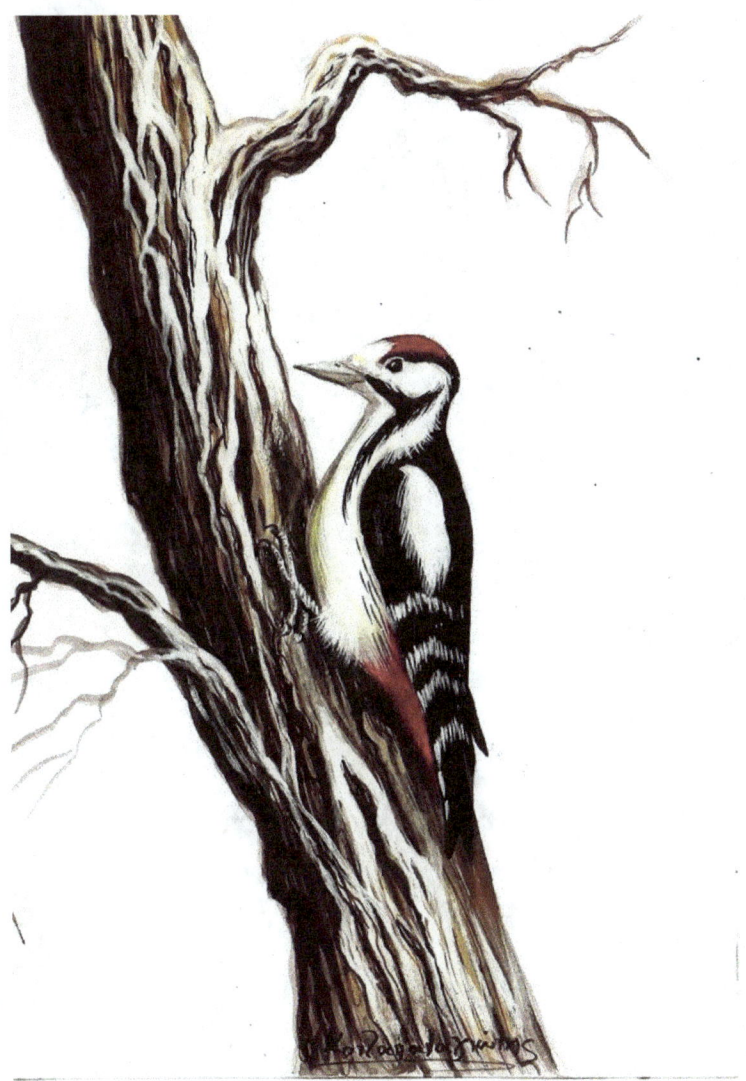

Drawings of wild animals

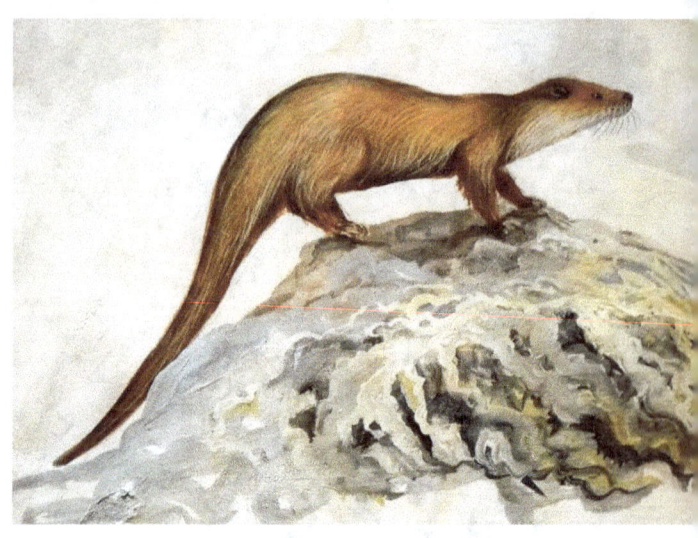

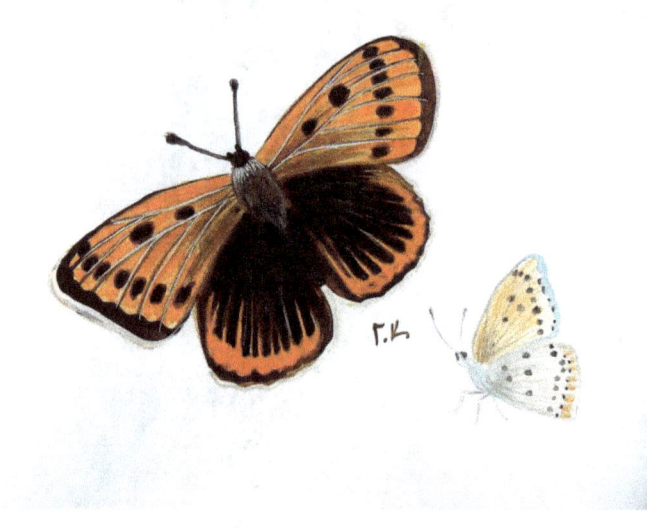

Drawings of wild animal

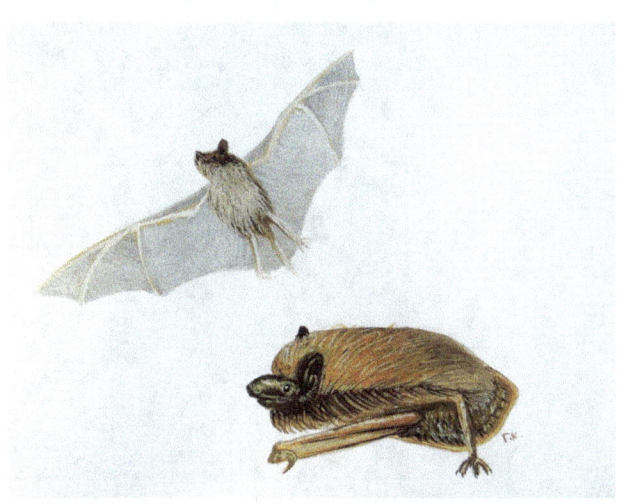

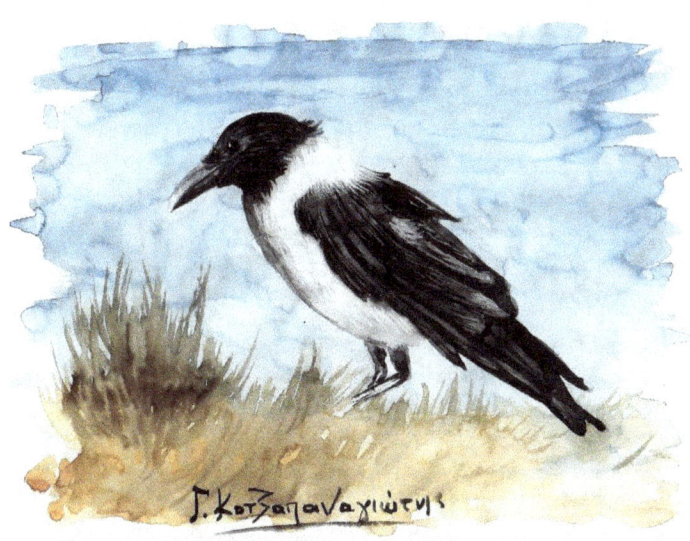

Face painting with oil colours

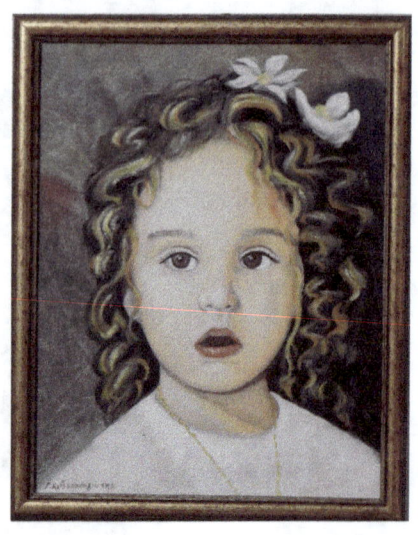

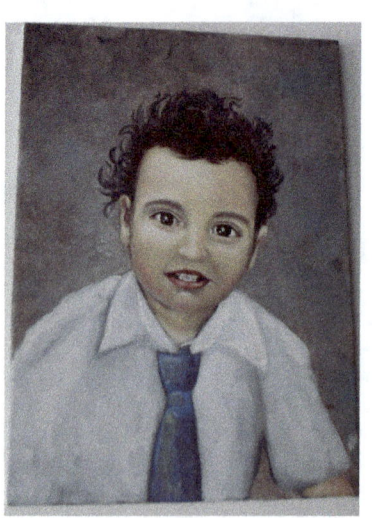

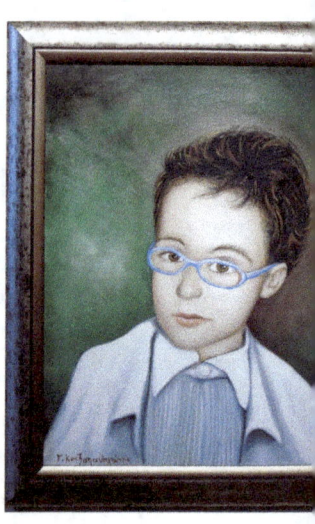

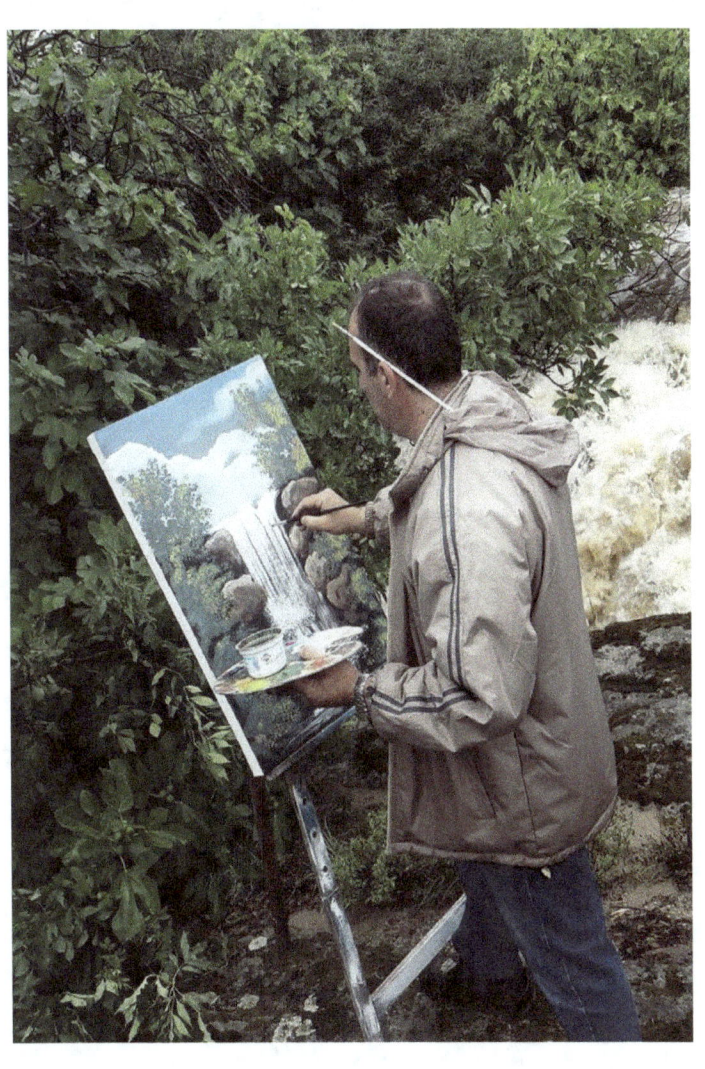

Outdoor painting

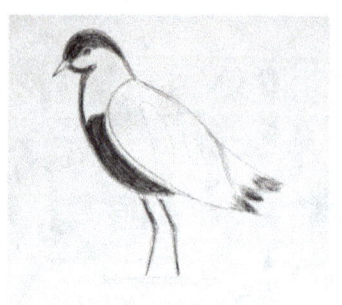

Drawings of wild animals

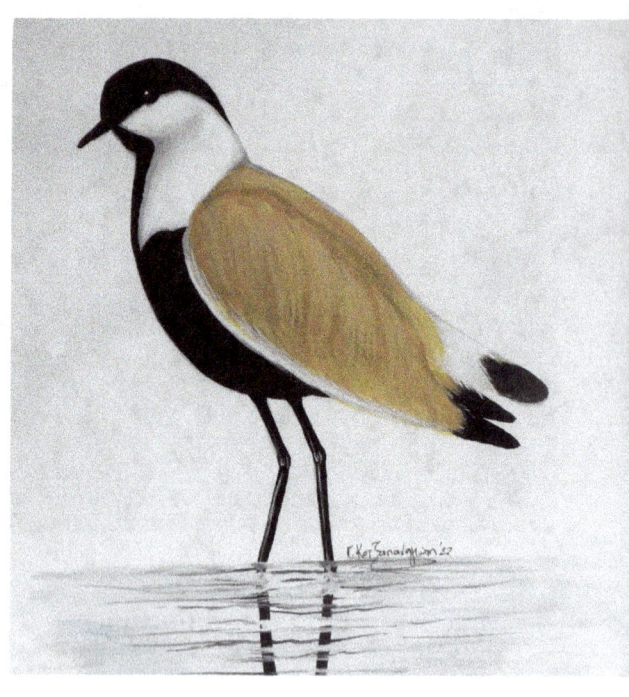

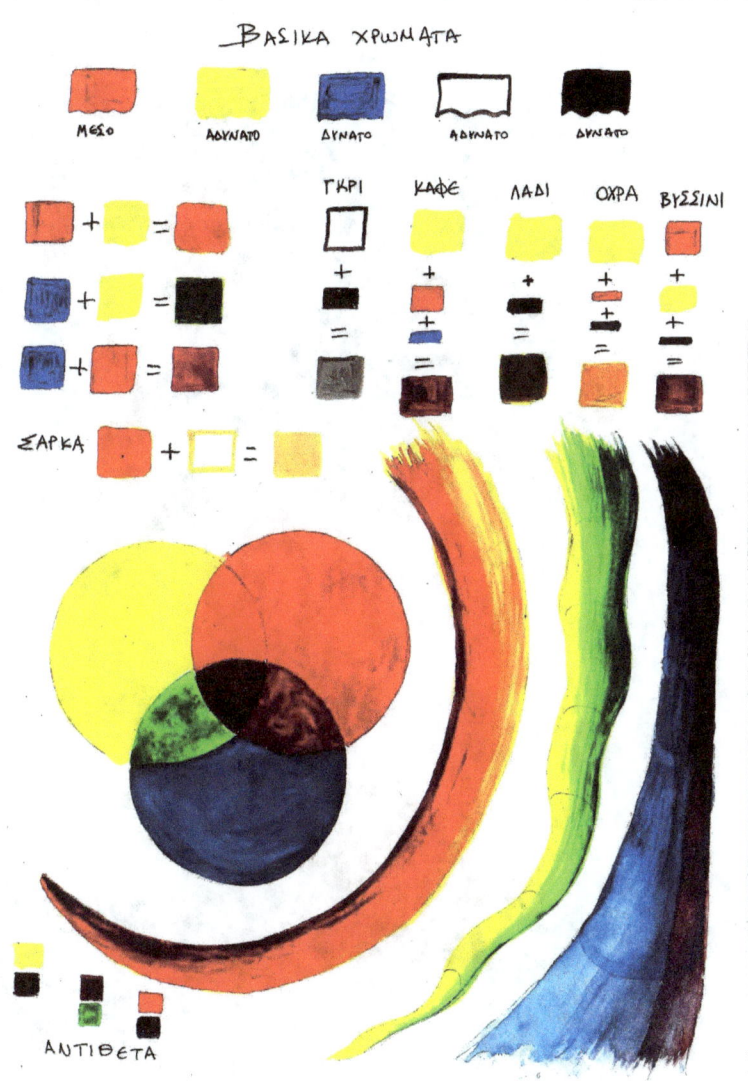

ΒΑΣΙΚΑ ΧΡΩΜΑΤΑ

ΜΕΣΟ   ΑΔΥΝΑΤΟ   ΔΥΝΑΤΟ   ΑΔΥΝΑΤΟ   ΔΥΝΑΤΟ

ΓΚΡΙ   ΚΑΦΕ   ΛΑΔΙ   ΟΧΡΑ   ΒΥΣΣΙΝΙ

ΣΑΡΚΑ

ΑΝΤΙΘΕΤΑ

Drawings of wild animals

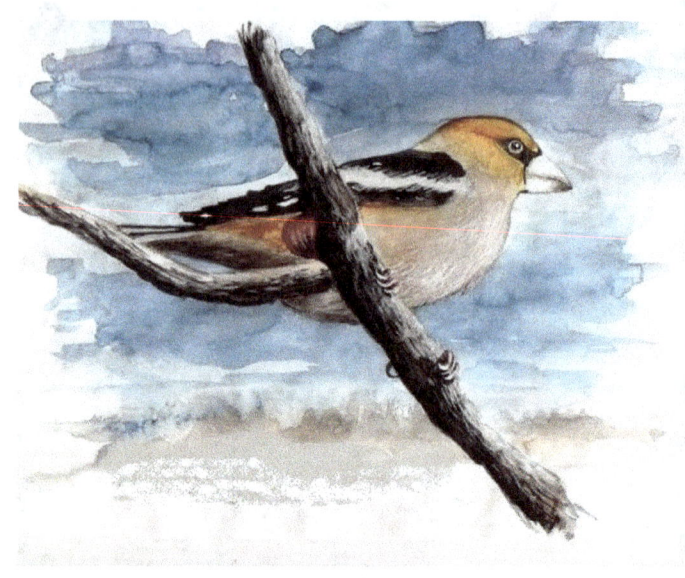

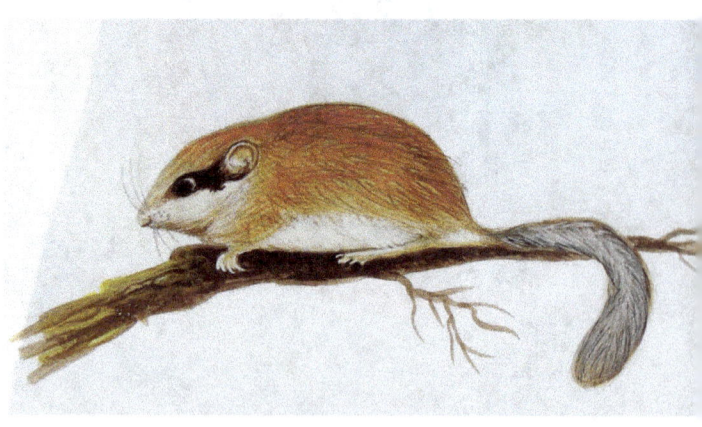

Drawings of wild animals

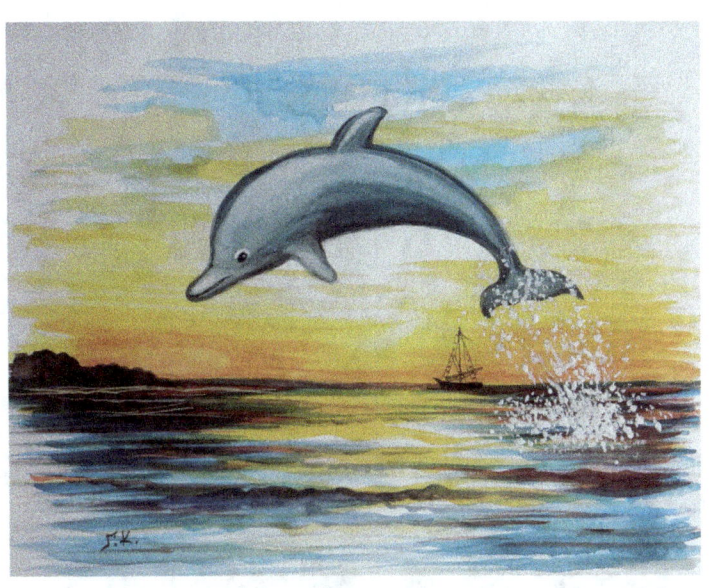

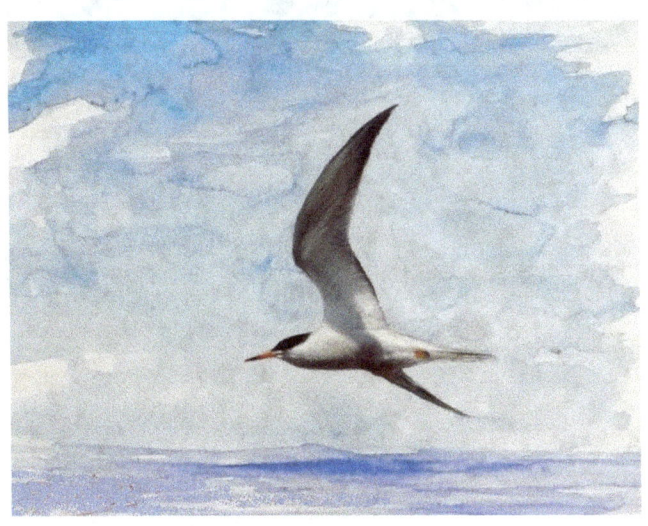

Landscape painting with a palette knife

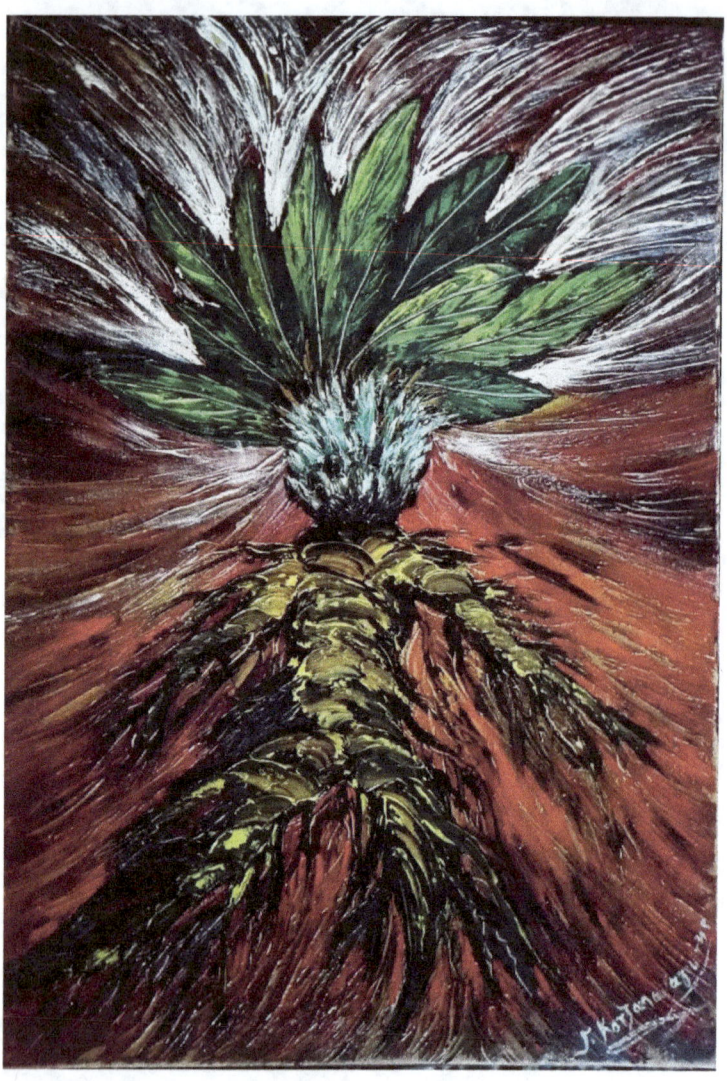

Painting on canvas

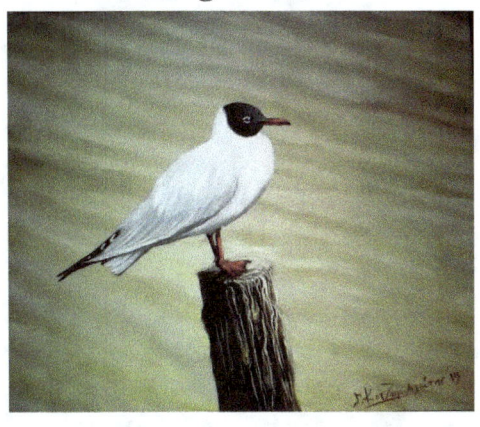

Painting for a theatrical performance on wood

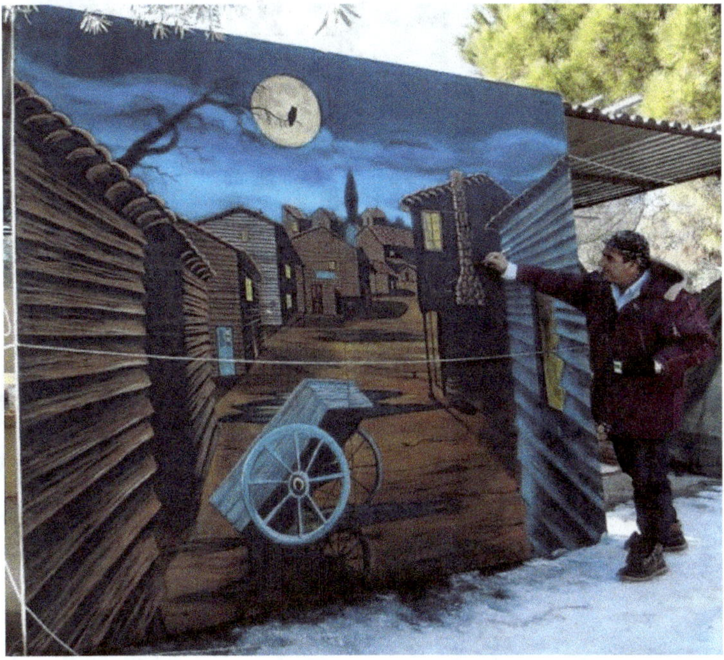

Styrofoam painting for a theatrical performance

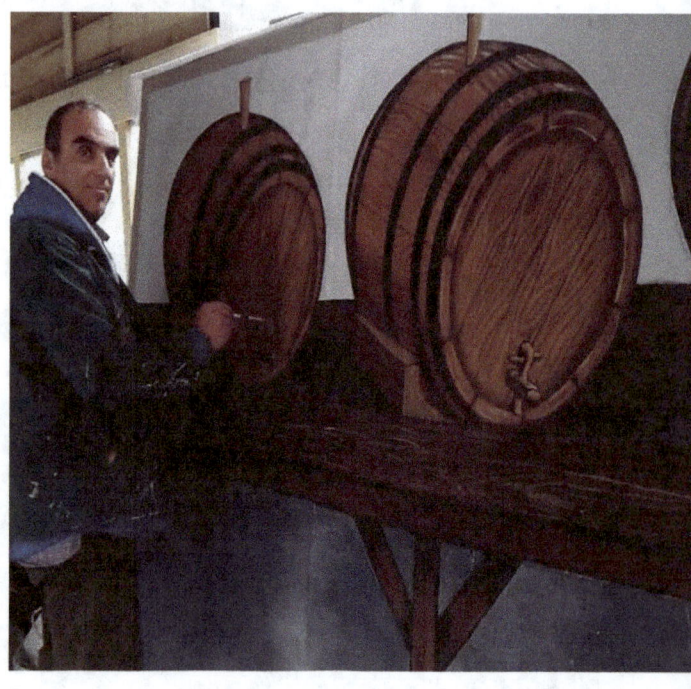

these pages you can practice. Take a pencil, eraser, sharpener and start drawing. We don't get frustrated with mistakes but move on to the next project.
You can also think of your own designs with each letter and number

these pages you can practice. Take a pencil, eraser, sharpener and start drawing. We don't get frustrated with mistakes but move on to the next project.

You can also think of your own designs with each letter and number